SWINDON
MOUNTAIN

For Jack

SWINDON MOUNTAIN

HARRIET HITCHEN

Crumps Barn Studio

ALSO BY HARRIET HITCHEN

NOVELS
nude
Swindon Mountain

SHORT STORY ANTHOLOGIES
Spooky Ambiguous
Festival of Cats
The Wild Night Sky

Crumps Barn Studio
Syde, Cheltenham GL53 9PN
www.crumpsbarnstudio.co.uk

Cover design by Lorna Gray
Illustrations © the author

Typeset in Adobe Garamond Pro

All our books are printed on responsibly sourced paper from a mixture of managed woodlands and recycled material. Printed in the UK by CMP, Poole.

ISBN 978-1-915067-64-7

Uffington Castle (hillfort) & White Horse

Wayland's Smithy (long barrow)

Swindon Mountain

Sketch of north facing elevation of Marlborough Downs identifying principal heritage assets and city of Swindon

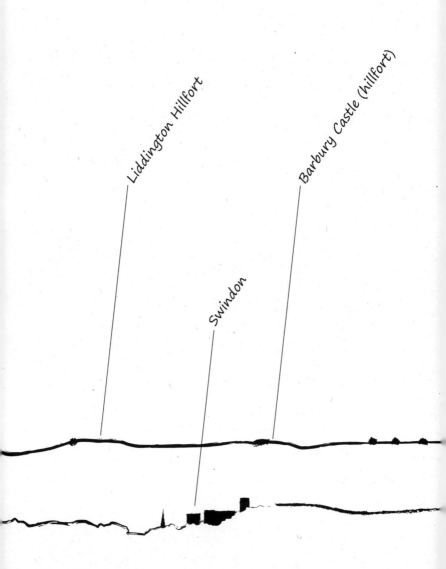

Liddington Hillfort

Barbury Castle (hillfort)

Swindon

Five months in and this soaring monolith, which a government source has privately dubbed a 'blithering inconvenience made out of rocks and mystery', is no closer to revealing its secrets

Brian Williams, journalist

I have heard a raven sing, so do not tell me that a mountain cannot simply appear.

I'm working in the largest of a hastily assembled network of portacabins in the shelter of the old farmyard at Castle Farm. Outside, the slopes are soaring above me in shades of cream and grey because chalk and limestone don't glow the same in rain.

There's a murmur of conversation in the meeting room next door. I think it's supposed to be soundproofed, but it isn't. I can hear the man who is here from one of the main heritage bodies – James – and a reply from Agatha. She's only my age but significantly more high-powered; she's the planning consultant who is really in charge of this project. There are eight people in there and they're trying to help someone else who's struggling to join them on Teams – probably someone truly high-flying, such as the Home Secretary, or a senior civil servant. It's scary what I overhear sometimes.

I should make it clear that I signed the Official Secrets Act. We all did. So I'm not really writing this; I'm not a specialist, and I'm not betraying other people's secrets. I'm just me.

We'd better bring Clare back into the office.

There was something about the way in which those words were spoken which has power. They weren't even uttered in relation to this project. As it happens, those words were said by David the senior manager at Ultimate Archaeological Services (UAS) to his colleague over a year ago for a different project, when they were desperately short of illustrators for a different reason, and he thought that I – with all my years of familiarity with their way of doing things – would be able to step relatively smoothly back into place.

It was the air of entitlement that raised my hackles. Or perhaps the easy assumption that I had no life beyond the company, and I'd never really left.

But I *had* left.

For me, the penalty for refusing to go along with their plan was a sudden severance of the occasional flow of freelance work that had previously been a lifebuoy for my meagre finances. Not even a small desk-based assessment – it was meant to be a reprimand.

But actually, I didn't really care. For me, the lasting legacy from that time is the sense of a life lived in parallel: the knowledge that I did not meekly agree to take the path they offered me, and a feeling like a memory of what life might be like if I had.

It's the same feeling I have about the moment when the

mountain appeared.

There was a time before it was there, and a time afterwards. But there was also the sense of possibility that it had always been there, or never had.

In official accounts, descriptions will probably begin with the appearance of the original landscape. Industrial Swindon rests on the edge of the wide floodplains near the source of the River Thames. The city has its back to the high ridge of the Marlborough Downs. They rise like a spine running east-west between London and the Bristol Channel. Geologically speaking, one of the highest points on this line of hills is – or was – to the east of the city, rising to about 260m above sea level. Prehistoric people saw the same value in high ground and built a long barrow there to haunt the hills with myths about their dead. Later, a tribe of horse people carved a giant white horse into the hillside nearby, presumably a signpost for their place amongst the living.

My experience of the landscape begins at home. Years ago, when I had a regular commute to the office, I used to drive about twenty miles from my rented cottage in the neighbouring Cotswold Hills towards Swindon. I still do, whenever I need to do a supermarket run. There is a point where the dual carriageway cuts south over the highest ground. From there, for a brief run of seconds, I am treated to a view from the rolling Cotswolds all the way across the floodplain to the vast grey wall on the horizon with its silhouette of three distinctive clumps of trees and the longer stretch of woodland which traces the line of the ancient ridgeway.

The long barrow is there, named Wayland's Smithy.

The mountain appeared overnight behind that ridge. It arrived five months ago without fuss or storm or earthquake. It straddles the boundary demarking Oxfordshire and West Berkshire, climbing to a rough craggy summit. They measured its altitude and it comes in at about 783m above sea level.

Its summit is limestone, so it is not volcanic – there is no charismatic slate and granite here like Yr Wyddfa. Nor is it an Everest of southern England, raised by friction between continents – there are no active fault lines between tectonic plates, so nothing to collide.

That was in February.

Eight weeks ago, as the hawthorn flowers were bursting into bloom, the phone rang while I was out walking. When I saw the caller ID, I had one of those momentary hesitations that fall between self-preservation and knowing that you've already made your decision.

Like I say, it's a little bit like a life lived in parallel, a point of divergence; except that I don't believe in parallel lives. There is no parallel reality where I agreed all those months ago to give up my newfound liberty in the land of self-employment to return to the office. I simply don't think there ever was a choice at that moment, because if there really was another path I might have taken, I'd already be doing it.

It's closer to the time I was contemplating moving to France but slightly accidentally decided to buy a horse instead. Or the time I was thinking of moving northwards to be closer to my parents, when the mountain arrived.

It shouldn't actually be called Swindon Mountain, by the way. It rises from Lambourn Downs and there is a hamlet called Upper Lambourn on the lower slopes with its larger neighbour Lambourn village just beyond, both of which are in Berkshire – but I suppose that wasn't poetic enough for the first news outlets that covered the story.

They've always treated Swindon a bit like Slough. A newspaper printed a cartoon John Betjeman penning a poem *Come friendly boulders fall on Swindon,* and that was that.

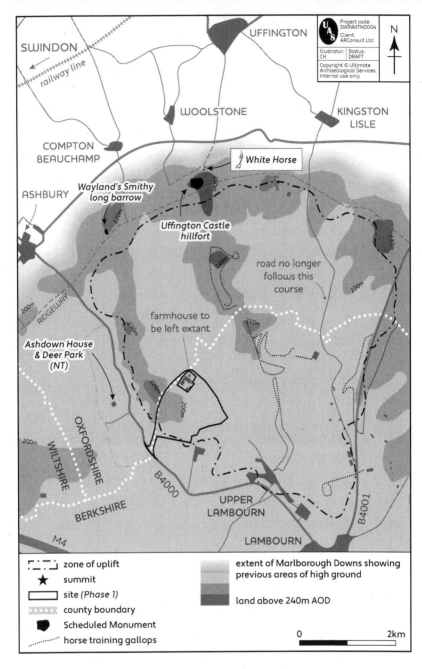

N

SWINDON

railway line

UFFINGTON

WOOLSTONE

KINGSTON
LISLE

COMPTON
BEAUCHAMP

White Horse

ASHBURY

Wayland's Smithy
long barrow

Uffington Castle
hillfort

road no longer
follows this
course

RIDGEWAY

farmhouse to
be left extant

Ashdown House
& Deer Park
(NT)

OXFORDSHIRE

WILTSHIRE

BERKSHIRE

B4000

UPPER
LAMBOURN

B4001

M4

LAMBOURN

zone of uplift

★ summit

site *(Phase 1)*

county boundary

Scheduled Monument

horse training gallops

extent of Marlborough Downs showing
previous areas of high ground

land above 240m AOD

0   2km

Location of the site, showing former areas of high ground
(scale 1:75,000)

2

I'm here at what is being termed 'basecamp'. The lanes are jammed with abandoned cars, and you can see behind me the queue as more people keep coming. With local services stretched to breaking point, the communities of Lambourn and Upper Lambourn are asking – how long can this continue?

Rebecca Morrison, journalist

There is a meeting going on in the room next door again. It still feels very surreal to be here. The mountain outside my window doesn't have that raw look of freshly hewn rock – the lower slopes are dotted with sheep, and from my desk I can see the golden flowers of gorse in a crevice higher up. When I agreed to take this job, I imagined it would be a daily commute to the usual office. They quickly disillusioned me about that. This was to be my first experience, after fifteen years of professional life as an archaeological illustrator, of working in the field.

But despite all the fuss they made about the necessity of being embedded in the away team, and the impossibility of personally commuting the twenty-four miles from my home to this location on a daily basis, my role is office-based. I spend a minimum of eight hours a day alone in this bland prefab cabin hunched over a computer screen creating maps that show the latest results from the field, matching them to the existing data. I feel sometimes as if I'm getting through day by day of this mad experience by sheer numb grit.

Once or twice a week, I listen to the murmur of voices through the thin partition wall. Agatha, James and a few others are in there now and it's an odd kind of companionship.

I feel as if we're connected even though we barely speak.

At this moment, I can hear the murmur of James's voice. He's talking to David – my boss, the senior manager who struck me from the freelance list – who is explaining that we nearly had an invasion of metal detectorists on site last night. David is speaking on Teams, because apparently the embargo on remote working doesn't apply to him. His voice pops up whenever we have a crisis, which is often. There was a protest at the gate this morning. There is a crowd on most days, but each one seems to be larger than the one which has gone before, and today's was worse than most.

It's because someone has started the rumour that the mountain was caused by a fracking accident.

Another voice on Teams is saying, "I can safely deny the reports? This isn't a case of plausible deniability – I really am asking. I'd like to be certain."

"I understand." Agatha is always calm and in control. I guess she's practised this with the enquiries into HS2, the Stonehenge Tunnel and the feasibility study for the River Severn Tidal Barrage. She represents one of the largest planning consultancies in the UK. "There are no recorded fracking sites in the vicinity."

Another voice adds, "There wouldn't be. There has been

a nationwide ban on fracking in place for several years, and the nearest historic location would have been Hampshire, or Somerset."

"So definitely not a fracking bubble?"

Don't swear, I mutter to myself. *Fracking this, fracking that* … Potty mouthed government ministers.

Nobody in the room shares my sense of humour.

Very seriously, Agatha replies, "The original seismic survey indicated that the limestone formation is substantial. Nothing has occurred to change that position. It isn't hollow."

"Good job," says David, "Since we now have a team of archaeologists undertaking a fieldwalking survey on the east slope. If we thought the mountain would just deflate beneath them like a balloon …"

"Yes, thank you David."

The first geological report is on my desk – the one they did long before there was even any talk about archaeology – so I know the mountain is made of oolitic limestone, with formations of clay, greenstone, chalk, silicified sandstone, and various soils. I'm familiar with oolitic limestone because the Cotswolds is made of it. There is apparently a notable outcrop running someway west of here in a diagonal stripe all the way from Portland Bill in Dorset, through the Cotswolds and underneath my home, and onwards up into Lincolnshire – the report declines to state with any certainty whether our mountain is formed of the same limestone. I also know that the report declines to confirm the age of the mountain or give specifics about how it was formed because *this falls outside the scope of the present investigation.*

This is one of those phrases which used to crop up a lot

in my life at one time. It's a go-to term for archaeologists, geologists and ecologists and all the rest involved in the planning system when something more might be known, but the client doesn't want to pay for further research, or won't like the answers.

I smile to myself. Freelance illustrators don't tend to have this limitation. Normally people want as much as they can get from me.

"So will I be correct if we put a line in the PM's statement to say it's consistent with the sort of rock which *ought* to be around there?"

"Sir Graham is probably the best person to advise you on this, Victoria."

I realise then that the speaker on Teams is Victoria Pearson, Press Secretary to the PM. There truly are some conversations someone of my paygrade shouldn't be party to. They really ought to sort out their soundproofing.

There is a hesitation. I'm well aware that the government's lead geologist is a bit of a liability. He has unrivalled credentials but his latest press conference was a disaster. At the end of his briefing about the stability of the slopes above the various populated areas, it came out that his background was oil and gas exploration. His last major contract was in the North Sea with Shell.

It is easy to imagine how the line of questioning ran from a tentative query about his interest in the site, to the ongoing mystery of the mountain's origins and from there to the present situation where there are protests outside the gate and the press secretary is scrambling to prepare a statement on fracking accidents.

"Can you summarise?"

"Geologically speaking, the limestone formation would classify as an uplift." This is from James. "Sir Graham's best explanation is that it is part of a sedimentary layer which predates the chalk. Perhaps a tilt occurred, or a fold, to thrust it up through the later deposits. This limestone formation has gradually become more prominent due to later erosion, becoming the mountain we know today."

"An island."

"Precisely. But Sir Graham felt it was important to make clear that this event is not commonly found in chalk downlands. As you can see in the chart before you, chalk is one of the relative newcomers to the geological scene. To put things in colloquial terms, it was laid down in the Cretaceous period by billions of dead plankton when this area was the bottom of a tropical sea. If we were to examine the geological column of the original downs – basically drop an imaginary shaft through the chalk to look beneath – we'd find that there are various clays and sandstones, which in turn are all underlain by a relatively thin formation of corallian limestone. These all represent various ocean floors."

"And below that?"

"An extremely thick formation of Oxford clay. And below that, mudstone which is a deep sea formation. And heading down further, oolitic limestone formations which are connected to the Cotswold Hills, with the lias group below that, which consists of mixed mudstones, clays and limestones. Incidentally, the oolitic limestone rises to a maximum height of 330 metres above sea level in the Cotswolds – but it sinks to almost 2000 metres below sea level near Portsmouth. It's all set on an impressive tilt. It's already deep underground by the time it passes under this area."

"So, let me be clear. What you're saying – what he's saying – is that there was already oolitic limestone in this area."

"Sir Graham hypothesises that the outcrop here may have been part of the formation which underlies our chalk downs, and that it was raised by the same forces which created the Weald-Artois Anticline."

"The *what?*"

"A shockwave from the collision between continents that formed the Alps." James has been much quieter of late. He used to stand out amongst them for his easy-going humour. "The shockwave became a ripple about 15 to 25 million years ago and raised the chalk downs across northern France and into the South East below London. He's suggesting that this limestone layer emerged like a splinter during that process. It's tougher than the surrounding layers, so it has remained while they have been worn away."

Agatha adds, "He's saying our mountain is millions of years old. *It has been here* for over 15 million years—"

The voice on Teams is incredulous. "Which in case you hadn't noticed is *slightly* at odds with what the rest of the known world is saying."

"This is why we aren't letting him do any more press conferences for the time being."

I smile into the screen of my computer. It's interesting to hear the tone of James's voice as he relays the information from the geology report. He's a scientific advisor who normally works closely with the County Archaeologist who in turn advises the planning committee on the county council, so he's here both as a source of support to ensure that the field teams know they're doing things properly, and also as a brake if he feels things are being rushed. It isn't his job to provide the most positive gloss to the PR team.

So I think the fact he's the one who's been delving into the substance of the geologist's report is an indication of his impatience when things aren't being done properly. In fact, his seriousness is similar to that moment ten days ago when he unexpectedly spoke to me on my side of the meeting room wall to inform me that they were moving all the archaeologists from our accommodation in the nearby village of Lambourn onto site. That task wasn't his job either.

A video had emerged on social media of one of the site team excavating what looked like an enormous spinal column. We all knew who it was because they were swiftly sacked, but the as-yet-unnamed archaeologist who took the clip sent it to a friend via WhatsApp, and somehow from there it leaked onto Instagram and then it ran everywhere.

By the time James spoke to me, David had already paid one of his rare visits to call a meeting with the field staff – not in the meeting room, there were too many of us for that – to find out who had shared the clip and remind us in the strictest terms about client confidentiality. There were also protests outside the gate. The crowds had been there all along of course – present in the background of every news sequence that showed us inching our cars through the gates while a reporter delivered the latest update. But suddenly the mood out there was significantly more hostile when we went back to our scattering of nighttime roosts in the village.

I don't think the senior managers had really grasped that this site was different from what was generally termed an *away dig*.

We were stuffed into any spare bedroom UAS could find because all the holiday lets and Airbnbs had already been taken by the swarm of press and fanatics who'd moved in long ago. And I should add that it was only the archaeologists who were having to live like this. Agatha, James and the rest of the consultants were only expected to travel here once or twice a week, so they were trusted to sleep in their own beds. They still are.

James's conversation with me came as the mountain was sinking beneath a low cloud, the coordinates I was trying to match with some site plans were wildly off the mark, and my car had been mildly vandalised.

"The move onto site will save you the commute at least. Were you able to get on site OK this morning?" It was strange to find him hovering beside my desk rather than simply passing through with the usual hello or farewell.

"Oh it was fine. And besides, the move will certainly be an improvement on the solitary splendour of my attic room in a 1950s terrace."

"You're lonely?"

"Hungry. I don't really dare to cook in the family kitchen."

For some reason, I didn't want to give the impression I was complaining – and anyway, my car was targeted by stealth while it was parked on the road in the dead of night, not by the crush of people at the gate that morning.

Viewing the fuss about the video from the inside, the

pattern of hysteria was fascinating. There was the initial hubbub about the discovery, embarrassing enough for UAS when it immediately made the local news, but the real momentum got under way when influencers and commentators began sharing remixes of the clip in an attempt to identify the monster. Very early on they agreed that with such a long run of interlocking vertebrae, it was clearly reptilian, long-necked, perhaps a tenuous match for a plesiosaur.

Then someone raised the point that the vertebrae had emerged from the ground in a condition where each piece was remarkably unfused, which was suspicious for a fossil. The evidence was clear – this was the articulated skeleton of a recently deceased monster.

Within twenty-four hours, the UK book trade sold out of all editions of Sir Arthur Conan Doyle's *The Lost World*.

Less pleasantly, the parallel world theory gained sway – the one where the mountain came from an anomaly which had briefly connected our world with an alternative earth where dinosaurs were still the dominant species.

The pubic began to fearfully revisit the official narrative of some incidents from the early days on the mountain. A frenzy of cyberstalking dredged up the names of the lead field archaeologists and even my face made it onto social media in a clip taken from one of the news reports at the gate one morning.

Perhaps there had been a government coverup. Perhaps we were part of it.

Perhaps the government had acted in an attempt to contain an invasion.

Was it, in fact, already too late?

The spinal column was a coral fossil. It is presently living on the end of my desk, labelled and bagged ready for a PR event with the local museum. The carelessness with the WhatsApp video came about because archaeologists don't actually have much to do with fossils. Despite the long history of newspaper headlines shouting *Call in the Archaeologists* whenever a dinosaur happens to be found, an archaeologist's job is the study of human activity.

For fossil identification, you need a palaeontologist, and the person we called identified this set of interlocking segments as the fossil of a sea sponge colony.

It *does* look like vertebrae, but there is no central channel where the nervous system would go. They're common in Cotswold limestone apparently, formed when the land beneath my home was the bottom of a shallow sea near the equator and a vibrant coral reef. Modern surface water can gently erode the softer rock away, leaving it neatly deposited within a wider area of rocks and hillwash.

Now there is a crowd outside the gates, I'm sleeping at night within metres of every other archaeologist in a hastily erected cluster of interlocking structures – which look like a barracks and don't help defuse things out there – and in the meeting room next door they're struggling to find the words to talk about 160 million-year-old limestone in a way that will refute the present fracking theory.

That last detail is why I ended up sidestepping James's questions about my car that day and admitted instead that the part I truly find hard to understand is not the mountain;

it isn't even the strangeness of being here.

It's the *slow pace* of change involved in making a great lump of limestone like that in the first place.

As if to illustrate my point, the mountain occupies the whole view outside my window.

It's the fact that this whole region of England was originally a living seabed somewhere near the equator, and when we talk about the alternating layers of geology which were either deep sea formations or the bed of a shallow sea, we're basically observing that the sea level changed that much with each new era. And now those formations are jammed at a jaunty angle above the surface by movement of the earth's crust.

When that piece of sea sponge was drifting northwards, the map of the world looked very different. And when these chalk downs were raised above the sea, that process of uplift took many hundreds of thousands of years, a fraction of a millimetre at a time. Much, much later, when erosion became a more dominant force than the uplift, modern humans hadn't yet evolved.

Archaeology is all about feeling connected to the past, I went into this line of work for that very reason. I *am* capable of grasping the concept that the terrain I know wasn't always like this – but it is next to impossible to come to terms with the scale of change involved.

It's even harder to grasp that – the sudden arrival of a mountain notwithstanding – the land I have walked on all my life is still moving, and will rise and fall again in the future.

When I mentioned all this to James during that single conversation last week, he simply stared at me. Eventually he said, "You don't speak like an archaeologist."

"That's because I'm not one. I have a Fine Art background."

I caught the tail-end of the glance he gave me. It was as if he was afraid he'd discovered a fraud. "How on earth did you end up here?"

I'm always asked this, so my answer was well-rehearsed. "I went to art college because I knew it was my one chance to study painting, but I always knew I wouldn't be able to make it as an artist. So I decided from the age of about fifteen that I wanted to be an archaeological illustrator. I've always loved history," I finished rather feebly.

"We do tend to, if we go into archaeology."

"In my case, I did all the work experience I could while at uni and I was really lucky and got a job at UAS as soon as I graduated. I finally left about two years ago." I caught his questioning look so added, "I've set up on my own as a freelancer. Book illustration. Mainly children's books."

Then, for my own sake, I added slightly defensively, "David, my once and present boss, always used to wonder if he ought to send me out to site sometime, so that I could learn how the drawings I prepared were actually made. I never could seem to make him understand that I'm not an idiot – I may not be actually digging the features, but I should like to think I must have picked up one or two ideas of how it all works after all these years, wouldn't you say? But he never sent me anyway. I've never left the office, until now."

Like the perfect punchline, the view through my cabin window was rain-smeared and merely showed a grassy hillside streaked with the ruts the site vehicles had left.

By my desk, James only said, "Must be nice to be back at the day job after that time away."

It's funny really, how people act as if my life after I left the job was a blank void and I jumped at the chance to come back because this is where I belong. Even him, and he doesn't even know me.

Apparently however, I don't know him either. It was some days after that stilted conversation that I discovered from one of the field archaeologists that while he was asking me whether I was coping with the pressure, he was having his life picked apart by the people out there for evidence he was secretly working for the MOD.

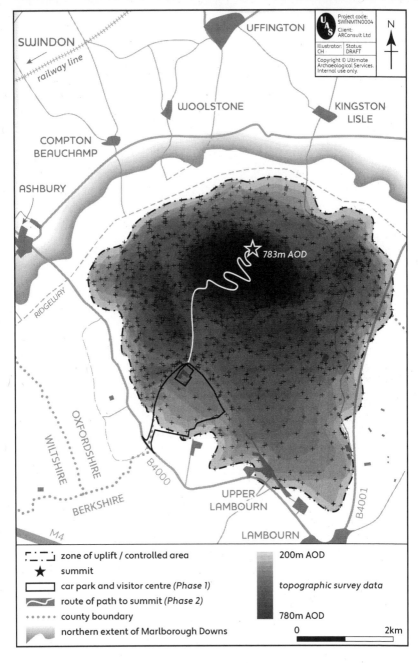

N

SWINDON

UFFINGTON

railway line

WOOLSTONE

KINGSTON LISLE

COMPTON BEAUCHAMP

ASHBURY

783m AOD

RIDGEWAY

OXFORDSHIRE

WILTSHIRE

BERKSHIRE

B4000

M4

UPPER LAMBOURN

B4001

LAMBOURN

zone of uplift / controlled area

★ summit

car park and visitor centre *(Phase 1)*

route of path to summit *(Phase 2)*

county boundary

northern extent of Marlborough Downs

200m AOD

topographic survey data

780m AOD

0   2km

Plan showing location of Phase 1 and Phase 2,
and topographic survey results (scale 1:75,000)

3

Pressure is mounting on the Defence secretary to deliver a robust response to what has been described by an inside source as 'blatant obfuscation by the Russian President'. All that remains is to ask – do the Russians have weapons capable of this? Are we under attack?

Jonathan Terry, political correspondent,
outside Number 10 Downing Street

I don't think anyone actually knows who first conquered the summit. There was no detectable scientific expedition, there was a stampede. Rising to 783m above sea level, the mountain might be climbed within three hours by a fit walker. Everybody waited a few days in a numb sort of shock; then by the following weekend, over 1000 people had set foot on the slopes. Another week later it was 10,000. By the fourth week, nearly 350,000 people had climbed to the summit.

Just to put it in context, the figure dwarfs the number of people who crowded onto Yr Wyddfa during the exercise-in-open-air phase of managing Covid.

This was possibly because, when the mountain first

appeared, the government dubbed it a local issue. It was up to the county councils and charities to manage things. A few retorts were flung back and forth during Prime Minister's Questions about *making mountains out of molehills,* but that was the end of the PM's interest. I also think the government saw the local name Swindon and felt a spasm of social judgement. I know I have the benefit of hindsight, but it was a bit like their response to the Grenfell Tower disaster – I don't think they quite grasped how clearly the public was expecting some form of national disaster response team to swing into action rather than local charities picking up the tab.

I remember the news footage of the cars blocking the pavements in the nearby village of Lambourn. There was no waymarked path, so people charted their own routes to the top. Everybody was disgusted, nobody did anything. The different county councils – Berkshire, Wiltshire and Oxfordshire – the charities, and local police force were overwhelmed. Someone made a clip of an elderly resident go viral, ranting on her doorstep.

In reality, I suspect the government was relentlessly peddling its harmless novelty angle to the public in an effort to stave off panic.

One of the most enduring images from the very early days is the clip of the Defence secretary on breakfast TV. He later became a meme for someone completely poleaxed by a sudden question. He was confronted live on air when he was trying to prop up his PM on a completely unrelated issue.

Defence secretary: *What I'm saying here is that we are regularly approached by lobbying groups for the energy industry. It is perfectly normal for the Prime Minister to meet—*

Presenter 1: *Let's take a call from one of our viewers. Dave, what question do you have for our guest today?*

Viewer: *This is a simple one. Swindon Mountain. Did the Russians do it?*

Defence secretary: [barely audible spluttering] *I … don't … think … you can't … ask that …*

The PM had already gone on record to sum up the government's position on the oddity's origins, saying *if it looks like a dog, barks like a dog, it's a mountain* – but once The Russian Question got out and became the headline on a tabloid newspaper the very next day, everything escalated very quickly.

After all, we'd all seen the movies. An alien invasion. A satellite weapon perhaps. If a mountain could be raised from nothing overnight, it had to be *something*.

I can't imagine the Defence secretary ever dreamed that someday he would have to explain live on air while sitting on a couch on breakfast television that he did not believe we were being attacked with mountains, and he could not imagine what the proportionate response would be if we were.

Specialists at the British Geological Survey were dragged into press conferences to reiterate that none of their sensors had recorded traces of seismic activity in the area on the night in question. No earthquakes, no rumblings and no signs of sudden explosions. And despite a sudden flurry of panic overnight in Ispwich and then Nottingham, to date there have been no additional new mountains. Swindon Mountain is a lone anomaly.

The statement from the Russian government was an implausible denial, suitably mocking with a thin veneer of aggression, which I found reassuring in its way.

Nothing stops a fever of anxiety once it gets going though. The gaze of suspicion fell next upon the nearby military firing range on Salisbury Plain. The Chief of the General Staff looked particularly silly having to deny that our military had weapons that were technologically advanced enough to create landmasses. The counterargument was that of course he would say that, if the army had been testing an experimental weapon and experienced a misfire.

As it happens, the nuclear question was the easy one to answer because from the very first day geologists were testing for radiation. Behind the filibustering from the government, there was a quiet scramble to establish whether the mountain was the first hint of a larger volcanic eruption – perhaps formed like a bubble over molten lava. I know this because I have access to all sorts of sensitive information and the first geological report sits on my desk. The report explains that one of the ways to measure volcanic activity, along with seismographs and monitoring equipment, is that igneous rocks often contain trace elements which emit radiation. Testing the levels of radiation allowed specialists to be reasonably certain that the mountain was not a volcano. And

I know this because they decided to leave a Geiger counter in the corner of my office, just in case. I think it's supposed to be the mountain equivalent of a canary in a cage – I'm almost always working nearby so I'll notice if it does more than pass the occasional annoying click. Somewhere else on site, there is a hut that houses a rather more sophisticated set of sensors. Everybody says the mountain is not emitting radiation, but they still didn't let the senior illustrator at UAS take the job because she's pregnant.

But inert or not, mountains are still dangerous places.

People were climbing in an unstoppable swarm, even in bad weather. When the first deaths occurred in a crush on the north slope in the fifth week, everything changed. No evidence of dinosaur attacks, I hasten to add, whatever was said later, but suddenly the headlines, which had been a diverse mix of novelty and faux outrage, all coalesced into one screaming accusation levelled directly at the PM.

WHAT WILL IT TAKE TO MAKE YOU ACT?

Finally the government stepped in. It issued a scathing criticism of the local council's response and swept in to encircle the base with security fencing, with hired guards and dogs patrolling the boundary. It declined to take us onto a war footing, and notably the military declined to assume control of the mountain. Instead, because the government was still playing a game of play-it-down-to-the-hysterical-voting-public and they didn't want a running battle with trespassers making headlines for months and months, a multi-agency scheme was hastily put in place for a car park and visitor centre, with a laid path to the summit.

And because an archaeological assessment is an established part of any planning application, this is where UAS was called in.

It must be said that one of the reasons why Agatha and James always look a little tightly wound is because normally this sort of development project would undergo years of feasibility studies before anyone would even conceive of getting permission to begin groundworks. In this instance, that process was condensed to four months of desk-based work and a very private planning committee session.

And now here we were.

4

Beyond that farmhouse, we can just see the growing network of temporary cabins where, I am told, a team of experts are analysing the material recovered from the excavation. Out here by the gate, I am with environmental campaigners who say the government must do more to guarantee the protection of wildlife and nature

Sally MacIntyre, reporter

The mountain is eerily quiet today. I see it differently now that I'm living here. I see it out of hours.

I used to go for a hurried walk after tea around the village, head down, dodging the protesters and the journalists, with the giddying heights an ever-present mark in the corner of my eye. Now I go for a pre-dinner stroll around the lower slopes while the field archaeologists mill around getting their dinner and washing the soil from their skin. I used to nip home at the weekends. These days we're living on site and my car is standing forlorn in the parking area. We're supposed to use the buddy system if we want to leave site, for our safety. Most of us stay. My car is rather distinctive anyway thanks to its impromptu paint job and spiderweb cracks on the glass.

I head back to the camp. The site vehicles don't come this

way, so the close-cropped turf is reasonably uninterrupted except by clumps of bird's-foot trefoil and red clover. The botanists were here long before the archaeologists arrived on site. They had an exciting time scrambling up and down the mountain analysing the herbage as part of the rushed pre-planning stage. Most of the plants, to quote their report, *'are consistent with this altitude and terrain'.*

Jess, the botanist attached to ARConsult – the planning consultancy firm that Agatha belongs to – is still involved in this project. I pass her as I head towards the communal area. She doesn't sleep here. She's only been visiting today to meet with a botanist from Kew. The specialists at Kew Gardens have oversight here in the same way Heritage England oversees the archaeological works. Their brief is to ensure that mitigation is in place to protect the more vulnerable species which are threatened by the development, which is laughable really, because even if they find something truly rare, they are under pressure to agree that a few artificial habitats and a sign or two will count as sufficient protection. But most of all, I know they're each privately desperate to be the one to discover that as far as the plants are concerned, this mountain has uplifted some poor unfortunate lowland wildflower to the giddy heights.

"Any luck?" I ask her.

"None. All we've proved so far is that chalk downlands and limestone uplands fall broadly within the established range of many plant species – there aren't even a few sickly trees out of place at high altitude, and to be frank, the upland species we're seeing up there look like they've been settled in for generations. Those which require more specific conditions, they're only growing at the altitudes we'd expect them to grow. Establishing that there are genuine outliers," she adds, "will be the job of future botanists. Look out for the glut of PhDs about 10 years from now …"

"Have you been to the summit yet?"

"Have you?"

I shake my head. "The archaeologists say it's windy."

She laughs. "Blowing a gale. Take a good pair of boots when you go. And a rain mac for the wind chill."

I can't see it today but I know that when you get closer to the summit – which I am unlikely to achieve in my brief excursions at the end of the working day – the soil gives way to rough rock with small islands of growth in sheltered pockets, like any self-respecting mountain.

We wave to the old farmer who is still hanging on in his beleaguered farmhouse and then Lucy makes a move towards her car. She pauses in mid stride and turns to me, calling across the gravel.

"Don't tell anyone I said this, but I think what we are *really* doing here is the primary research of what the mountain actually is. The government doesn't care about giving the public access. It just sees this scheme as an easy way to shift the cost of investigating it all onto the private sector and heritage bodies."

Then she leans in conspiratorially and mock whispers, "Seriously, don't tell anyone I said that. These slopes have ears."

5

I am standing at the heart of one of the so-called Winterbournes – the villages which straddle this western face of the Marlborough Downs. They take their names from the springs here, which are known for flowing full and fast in the wettest months of the year, drying up in summer. Now, as you can see behind me, they are in full flow and we're in mid July. Residents tell me they're worried the mountain has had an effect on the water table.

Here with me is Wiltshire District Councillor Cynthia Hamish. Cynthia – people are concerned about flooding. What can you say to them? Are their homes at risk?

Well Gary, we're working closely with the Environment Agency to monitor—

**Gary Warbeck, journalist,
interviewing Councillor Cynthia Hamish**

My walk here takes me about thirty-five minutes. Nearly two miles without seeing another soul. At least out here, the absence of people is considered a boon rather than a problem. Behind me, the mountain wears a halo in the morning light. It casts a long shadow. The rumour-mill has a new theory today – that the mountain was caused by Climate Change. Last year, the South West of England had record rainfall and the idea is that we've experienced the opposite of a sinkhole, I presume, like a cork bobbling up from the pressure on a muddy bottle.

I like it as theories go. It has a contemporary edge. But out here on the north slope, this place doesn't seem alien enough to fit any theory. These fields were planted with crops before the mountain arrived, but they're still growing now. There is ripening barley around my seat. The artist in me thinks that if I were to paint this scene – and I won't, because I'm useless at landscapes – I'd paint the view from here. Or perhaps I'll just sit and enjoy the captivating vertigo of the plunge down to the ridgeway, and the step from there to the place where the original chalk downs fall dramatically away to the river valley as they always have.

The long barrow named Wayland's Smithy is below me on the ridgeway, or at least the ring of tall trees that surrounds it. The significance of the monument's position is so clear from here. It stands right on the edge of the downs, overlooking the wide span of the Thames valley bottom. I can see the massif of the Cotswolds – not the correct geological term, I know, but it fits how I feel – as an answering bulk on the distant horizon. It fills me with longing for my home.

I've noticed before now that the perimeter of the site is basically a set of compass points through time – on my way here I passed a 17th century deer park owned by the National Trust to the west; directly before me to the north, Wayland's Smithy dates from the later Stone Age; to my right, the

Uffington White Horse and the Iron Age hillfort are barely visible around the north-east curve of the mountain; and on the far side, out of sight from here of course, I know there is a pretty sizeable barrow cemetery from the Bronze Age – which is called Seven Barrows but really consists of roughly forty distinct burial mounds – while a long run of villages, businesses and houses that represent the medieval period to the present day robustly straddle the southern boundary.

The first time I walked here, I expected the city of Swindon to be closer. It's far off to the west. I can see the tiny cars moving along the main road but everything is gently fuzzy with morning haze.

It all seems so removed from reality. I'm expecting the field team to come back tonight with definitive proof at last that the archaeological record up there fits its new altitude, and we can all begin to accept that the mountain has always been here. Except we can't, because these crop fields were gently rolling hills only six months ago and I don't even know if a combine harvester could work on this incline. And Wayland's Smithy down there is a 5000 year old monument to death and hilltops, and if I'm honest, one of the most unknowable things of all here – except I'm pretty confident they were usually built on the high ground.

And this leads me to confess something. For a rather shorter time than 5000 years, my relationship with that monument has been limited to seeing it from the road near my home as an ever-present silhouette on the far horizon, just like the three distinctive stands of trees that dot the ridgeline further west.

On some days, back in the days of that tedious daily

commute to the office at UAS, usually when the light was right on a sunny morning with a hazy bank of cloud just like today, I'd leave my home in the Cotswolds and crest the high ground – and I'd catch a faint shape of a distant mountain rising behind this ridge.

It was an optical illusion. I know that. A trick of the eye. I don't actually have prescience – and the mirage rose slightly further to the west of here anyway, directly behind Swindon, near the place where those three distinctive clumps of trees mark the horizon.

But recently, in the time when I was working here but still allowed home at the weekends, I'd travel back on a Monday morning and I'd still sometimes see the mountain of my imagination. Except that now it seems like the real mountain's shadow.

Here, today, someone ruins the peace by moving on the mountainside below me. They're an unidentifiable black speck stumbling along the inside of the fence between the site and Wayland's Smithy. I check the time on my phone. It's probably a security guard on patrol. I'm not supposed to be up here anyway. It's the prompt I need to go to work.

As I go, a different black-clad sentinel breaks away from the hillside. There are raven here, just as there are near my home. But these birds just make the usual range of coughs and barks as they flap lazily into the space where the land falls away. I say good morning to them, but they give no sign of noticing me.

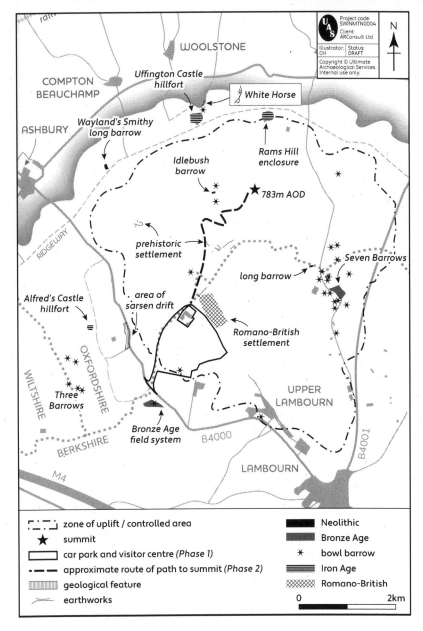

Prehistoric and Romano-British features from the known archaeological resource, depicted on the former cartographic data (scale 1:75,000)

6

While work begins on a new, previously unexplored, area on the east slope, a leaked memo from inside the camp indicates that archaeologists are growing increasingly concerned about 'nuclear' biosecurity measures. With no material being allowed off the site, we have to ask – are the public being misled about the dangers of a new pandemic?

Carole Ashford, online news journalist

We have a mole. We've been briefed yet again not to talk to the press. And in our communal area next to the kitchen, someone has scrawled on the large whiteboard:

Days since the last monster attack: 8

It is the date their colleague was sacked.

The rush in the kitchen has cleared. Archaeologists eat in waves. Now that the tide has ebbed, the few who are left are picking at the crumbs and the current topic for discussion is Agatha's management technique.

"Watch out, the troll'll be visiting us again tomorrow."

Ben is one of the hardened members of the field team. I seem have been absorbed into the huddle formed by the people who have worked at UAS for longer than I have. They either smile and then broadly ignore me, or treat me as a slightly vacuous but well-meaning tagalong – or perhaps that is just my insecurities speaking. The younger recruits don't seem to recognise me as someone to talk to at all. They see me as something *other*. Someone to be polite to, like a manager. Ben is universally liked. He's hovering in the doorway from one of the other rooms – the one with sports perpetually playing on the TV.

Someone sniggers. "Don't hold back. Say what you really think."

"It's like royalty visiting. Swooping in with her entourage and harassing us to work harder."

"And whatever you do—"

"Don't talk to the press!"

Kate, one of the real old-timers, shuffles into the room. "I heard she was the one who demanded that Archie was removed from site. For some WhatsApp clip he didn't even make. Stupid cow."

"Actually," I startled myself by speaking. "I'm not sure that's right."

Kate turns her gaze on me. She belongs to the third group – those who are so experienced and so immersed in fieldwork that they exist on a different plane entirely. She has absolutely nothing to say to me at all. If we're considering royalty, I think she and her ilk belong to that order.

And as Archie was one of her team, I can see why she might be taking things personally.

I say apologetically, "I overhear things sometimes. I'm not supposed to, but they meet in the office next to my desk.

I think it was David who said something about sending him home." Then it dawns on me that I'm not supposed to share the secrets of what goes on in that room. I'm stirring up trouble against our own management. Plus if school taught me anything, it was that one unguarded word in the middle of all their grumbling would inevitably be the single detail that would get reported back to the people in charge.

I add hastily, "I don't know though. I'm probably wrong."

Ben though is suddenly fascinated. "So you're our spy, Clare …" He grins as if my secret has been revealed. "How are you finding it in the office, working in close proximity with the dragon?"

I shrug. "She's fine. I think she's OK. She gave me a water cooler."

"Oh, well in that case …"

"She saved me from David. I was *admittedly* building up a tiny collection of mugs on my desk because I'd started taking a couple over each time to avoid having to trudge back to the welfare cabin every time I wanted to get a drink. David commented on the mess when he visited. Said it was inefficient."

"Hey Steve, Emma." Ben shouts back into the TV room. "What?"

"Did Agatha give you a water cooler?"

"We have a sink. And power. And enough foresight to bring a kettle when we came to set up the lab."

Steve and Emma are proof that we're taking things pretty seriously here. It is being reported out there in an alarmist sort of fashion that biosecurity measures are being ramped up on site, as if we've taken to wandering around in hazmat suits complete with breathing apparatus. It's nonsense of course. The field team wear hi-vis, work boots and hard hats, and if they're particularly conscientious, gloves, but that's as far as their concessions go towards health and safety. In fact, the only time I've ever seen an archaeologist recoil from a spot of dirt was when they uncovered a badger skeleton. It had been underground since Roman times, and TB pathogens can survive millennia.

But all that being said, the reports are right about one thing – the excavated material *is* being processed on site, rather than being sent back to the lab in the UAS office.

In fact, excavated material has never been taken off-site. We aren't stupid.

Even from my standpoint as a relative layperson, I can see it makes sense that they set up a finds officer and two environmental archaeologists with microscopes in a small lab in one of the other cabins. Notwithstanding the threat of finding that the parallel-earthers are right and we're unleashing off-world disasters upon an unsuspecting populace, it saves transporting the samples all around the country – which in turn means we will be able to stave off some inevitable future furore about outside contamination affecting the results.

One of the project officers, Niamh, blows on her cup of tea, clearly wishing it was a beer. She tips her head back on the sofa to peer at Kate. "Do you remember the site we did at Tewkesbury."

"The one with the fucking enormous ditch?"

"Phil couldn't find the bottom of his section."

"Phil was an idiot. When I started at UAS, he used to go

barefoot. Said it allowed him to *feel* the secrets of the land beneath his feet. Until he stubbed his toe on a rusty lump of metal and had to go to hospital in a panic about tetanus."

That was long before my arrival at UAS. Reminiscences are the bread and butter of conversation in the field team. They make excellent entertainment, but are not easy to contribute to.

I usually dive headlong into saying something earnest, such as the detail that even I'm required to wear site boots in my cabin. I'm gently creating a little muddy trail from the door to my desk and back again. I don't mean to seem so pathetically naïve. I'm actually trying to rationalise the slightly surreal map that is forming of my life on the carpet beneath my feet. The trail leads very clearly from the door to my desk, and there is a particularly dirty area beneath my chair. It's reached the point that I'm tempted to start laying new paths, by creeping along the wall perhaps, or by walking in loops on tiptoe, just to create some variety.

I look around at the field team and say nothing of course. I think if we all gave an account of being here, our lived experience of this site would seem very different.

"Hey Clare," says Ben. "What other choice titbits do you overhear in these meetings? Anything about the mysterious third area?"

"It's a quarry site," says Kate sharply as we all stare at her. Seniority clearly has its perks. Even I don't know this detail. "They're going to be extracting limestone. They're squeezing it through on the back of the public access project to appease the main landowner who is some Lord Something-or-other."

"Of course they are. Someone somewhere always has to

be making money somewhere along the line." This is from Niamh. *"Now* we know why the Government was so quick off the mark. I bet he's a party grandee."

"I know that," retorts Ben crossly. "I'm asking Clare what she's heard."

Theres's something sharper about his eyes when he's asking that. All archaeologists have a slight touch of the far horizon in their gaze – even archaeologists who have moved away from the field such as Emma or Steve, or even James – as if the memory of the harsh outdoors will forever whistle through their bones, but it isn't his manner that affects my reply. It's mine – it alarms me how pleased I am to be in the position of having something genuine to offer their conversation.

Impressively though, in the race to filter through all the things I shouldn't know, I only manage to smile under the weight of the sudden attention of all the people in the room, and say, "Mainly it's a spokesperson for the PM worrying about what conspiracy theory he should debunk in his next speech."

And since the PM is always blustering about something, that seems a pretty safe thing to say.

7

This morning we're at the National Trust's Ashdown House and deer park, which is separated from the mountain by a narrow valley. Beloved of dog walkers, these woods and meadows are home to a herd of fallow deer.

But this seemingly gentle valley also hides a secret...

The meadow behind me is strewn as far as the eye can see with large irregular grey boulders. This is what geologists call a 'Cenozoic silcrete drift' – the remains of a thin crust of rock which once covered this region.

It is known to the rest of us as sarsen stone.

Famously, these rocks supplied the enormous slabs which were revered for their special powers and dragged from a nearby woodland to be raised over 4500 years ago at Stonehenge.

We're now being told that sarsen stones are being found on the slopes of Swindon Mountain. To the pagan community and druids gathering in larger and larger numbers by the gates, this is just further proof that the mountain needs special protection. We're hearing increasing demands for access, and reassurance that this sacred site is being respected.

Heather, thank you for joining me. What is the mood
here at the mountain today?

Samia Himid, science correspondent

I can hear James's voice on the telephone in the next room.
The conversation doesn't seem to be going very well. There
are long silences as he listens, followed by tense phrases such
as, "I understand."

Agatha hasn't arrived yet. They'll be visiting the new
site on the east slope, which is to be a fieldwalking survey
covering several hectares. I wish I didn't know that it was a
quarry site. Or perhaps living in this environment of endless
conspiracy theories is catching, and being privy to secrets is
the real plague here.

I haven't seen any reports for that area yet and it's just a
big hatched polygon of blue on the masterplan called *Phase
3*. On my plan, the car park and visitor centre *(Phase 1)* are
outlined in red at the base of the south-west slope, beside our
basecamp and the farmhouse. The path to the summit rises
from there *(Phase 2)*.

It's easy to tell at a glance why they chose this option as
the preferred route to the summit. We're surrounded on all
sides by heritage assets, but here the car park will be largely
screened from the nearby deer park by a natural rise in the
ground, and the route to the summit stands a reasonable
chance of getting there without bulldozing anything vital.
The alternative would have been to run the route right out of

the back of the village of Lambourn, but I think the residents would have started a civil war over the increased traffic.

I'm trying to match the original drawings that were created in the UAS offices as part of the pre-planning process with the present data which is coming from site. They used what was previously known while we're working now with the real signs of occupation that are coming out of the ground. Archaeology is all about the little details – features such as pits or postholes are like shadows of past human lives, or a glimpse of something out of the corner of your eye.

As Jess the botanist says, our current job is to establish what evidence is present on the site. It is the job of the future to understand what it all means.

But none of it will count for anything, if we don't record it accurately.

"I know. I'm not disputing that." I can still hear James next door. He doesn't sound happy.

In my domain, things don't seem to be going much better. The old data simply doesn't match the new evidence.

I wasn't involved in the pre-planning work, although I have access to the files now. The consultancy team at the main office produced those illustrations. They searched out records of past excavations, earthwork surveys, cropmarks and historic maps, and plotted them on the modern mapping. With regards to the historic maps, they also had to warp them in minute ways to fit – a process called rectification – because bygone cartographers weren't quite as accurate as our modern survey techniques. All this was done for the pre-planning assessment so that they could state with some certainty where field boundaries were *likely* to be found.

Now I'm trying to do a variation of the same thing all over again to match the historic evidence with the real results we're finding in the field. And it isn't working.

The particular drawing I'm struggling with is a plan of a boundary just within the area of the future car park. It has been tentatively identified as a perfectly ordinary post-Enclosure field boundary based on its form and a few other clues such as pot sherds. The team has traced the extent of the feature using a GPS. They've generated a digital outline that on my screen looks like a glorified join-the-dots drawing.

The boundary ought to roughly match what we can see on the Tithe Map from 1845. This is a beautifully drawn map that marks out the newly enclosed fields around our farmhouse and adds key trackways and the wide open space of Lambourn Downs where this area was still predominantly unenclosed grazing. Just proving the point about the value of examining old maps, the earlier maps of this area such as the Rocque Map of 1761 show that there are no boundaries here, nor the farmhouse either. It was, apparently, a warren.

The problems for me begin with the fact that on the rectified version of the Title Map, the boundaries near this farm are gradually curving off their real alignment. The trackways slant left, a good way from their charted routes on the most recent Ordnance Survey mapping. It would be easy to dismiss the whole map as poorly measured nonsense.

But I don't. Despite the differences in technology between our era of mapping and theirs, and the fact, for example, they didn't have the ability to view their land from the air, it is generally astonishing how close these sorts of maps come. We even have some of the boundaries still present on the modern mapping to help us along. But in this crucial location they're barely matching at all. The GPS data is slightly – but fundamentally – misaligned. It cuts northwest, while the consultant's assessment would suggest our excavated feature falls on the lower of two parallel field boundaries which run precisely east-west.

Sometimes the alignment goes awry due to accuracy issues with the GPS. Mountain shadow, as the field staff are starting to call it.

Alternatively, it would be easy to assume that the issue is the sudden addition of a mountain on the scene. It wasn't there in 1845, after all.

But it isn't quite as simple as that.

Next door, I can hear him saying, "I'll get it done. I'll get it *done.*"

We have two forms of digital mapping in use at the moment. The original Ordnance Survey data for the hills and valleys around Wayland's Smithy. And the recent topographic survey of the mountain, which aligns with the GPS data we're getting in the field. Both I and the consultant used the most recent mapping, so at least I'm not stuck trying update a drawing that was based on the original OS mapping. But I could have worked with that anyway. For these lowland areas, it would simply be a case of correcting the tilt.

I think the consultant who prepared these pre-planning drawings forced a fit between the Tithe map and the modern boundaries. This is a method where you decide that certain points on the historic map absolutely represent certain coordinates, and the GIS software squashes and stretches the entire image so that they match. It's a perfectly accepted way of doing things, particularly when the surveyors of historic maps such as this Tithe Map seemed to run out of steam the further the fields were from the main settlement. I, however, take a different approach. I like to assume that the cartographers knew a thing or two about measuring, even if they didn't have the benefit of a birds-eye view. When I go back to the starting point and rectify the map myself, I like to keep the entire plan in proportion. I scale it by eye and rotate it fractionally until I achieve a best fit. Or at least I used to, before the mountain arrived. Now I also have to rotate the map on the vertical axis as well to make it match the new tilt of the land. Viewed from above, the historic map looks slightly squashed from top to bottom. But viewed in 3D so that I can rotate the view to achieve the original horizontal plane, the map has retained its proportions and its integrity. Those historic cartographers weren't entirely making things up.

Inevitably this looks less pretty than the consultant's version. But sometimes, as is happening now, the historic map throws up some interesting results.

Everyone has been working on the assumption that the long-lost boundary we've investigated is the southernmost one of two parallel lines. They're wrong. It's the northernmost one.

What does it truly matter, I hear you ask? All I've done is prove that the consultant made a small mistake and they picked the wrong grubbed-out 19th century field boundary. So what? Perhaps now I can tell myself that I'm terribly clever and spend a moment feeling insufferably smug about it.

But that's not the point at all. The issue is that if we can be wrong about the data from 1845, we can misplace the cropmarks from a Roman settlement visible on an aerial photograph. Or the data from a 1990s excavation for one of the racehorse stables. And what if those archaeologists made mistakes in their recording too? What if their site drawings have a Bronze Age field system in the wrong place and we're trying to match up a great big ditch which runs across their site into ours?

I've seen it happen before, and with significantly more important features than this little modern field boundary. I've mentioned it already and I'll say it again – it's the job of the archaeologists to uncover the evidence and interpret what they find.

It's my job to make sure the drawings are accurate.

Worrying about that detail may be making me a *little* stressed.

"Good heavens," says James from his doorway. "You are human after all."

I blink my way out of my thoughts and turn my head. "Pardon?"

"I'm sorry, I shouldn't have said that." Embarrassment flickers across his face.

"What?" I prompt.

"It's just that I've always wondered how you've managed to remain so unflappable while the rest of us are barely hanging by a thread. You always greet everyone with a cheerful *'Good morning!'* Today, you didn't."

I'm slightly perturbed by what is presumably an accurate impression of my voice. Then I realise that someone else is moving behind him in the meeting room. It's Marek, one of

Agatha's assistants, who must have stepped through the office while I was glowering at my screen.

James adds, "Is everything all right?"

I give in and show my amusement. Then I gesture at my screen. "Don't you think that the most surreal part of all this is that the old maps still fit? And the aerial photographs and the previous reports? The land is just on a different incline."

I click through the different layers. "The mountain ought to have forced its way up through the original landmasses like a splinter. Or it ought to have landed like a giant cowpat and smothered what was here before. Or perhaps it ought to have erupted from underneath like the spoil heap of a termite mound. What definitely shouldn't be the case is that when you zoom in on a specific area, the original boundaries and trackways are still present in a relatively unruffled state. They just *look* different in plan view because when you look at the land from above, you have to take into account the gradient. The boundaries haven't really changed."

I stop there. This is a bit like the day I gave him the unsolicited lecture about my struggle to match geology with the span of time. I don't know why I keep telling him things. But I can't help it. Perhaps it's because he's one of the only people of a high enough paygrade for me to be allowed to talk about these things without getting in trouble. And maps are fascinating. And he *ought* to be interested. He's our science advisor.

I turn back to my computer. I have the mapping in AutoCAD – a mapping system which plots in 3D. I can rotate the view like a spinning top and look at the surface of the mountain from underneath if I want to. Or simply adjust the view so that the field by our basecamp is more level, like it was before.

"Look at this," I say. "Just look. Rectifying the maps gets a bit tricky near the summit where we hit the rougher terrain higher up. There aren't enough traces of the old trackways to definitively match any boundaries up there. Plus, the tilt is all over the place and there's some stretch too. But as the soil quality improves, the trackways and boundaries broadly line up once more, and the lower slopes continue seamlessly on their original alignments. You just have to account for the new gradient."

I catch him staring at my screen and he's either working out how to extricate himself, or thinking through what I've found.

I plough on doggedly, "I know that if I go out there and *look* at the boundary, it'll be running over outcrops and gullies that weren't there before. I'm just saying that on plan, the boundaries haven't really changed."

"Try explaining that to the Second World War historians whose treasured decoy airfield over on the east slope has almost completely disappeared into an area of rockfall. Nobody would have believed for a moment that we were keeping a fleet of Spitfires on that terrain." His phone pings behind him on the meeting room table and he glances towards it and grimaces. "Or was that what you were heading off to look at yesterday morning?"

I stare at him blankly.

"You were wandering around the lower slopes."

Now I just look guilty.

"I'm just saying that I haven't seen you out there before."

"That was you? I thought it was a guard." I sit back in my seat with a laugh. "I normally go for a stroll in the evenings to get a bit of fresh air before tea, but the morning light lured me out before starting work yesterday. I don't normally walk in the mornings." I think I'm telling him this so that he knows I won't disturb him again.

"I suppose you haven't seen much of the mountain – they haven't taken you up to the current excavation area?"

This is getting rather too close to the time when David, back in the days when I worked full-time at the UAS office, arranged for me and the administrative team to go out on site for a day to *experience what really happens in the field* – as if most of the admin team weren't women who used to work in the field until they had children and needed kinder hours, or people like me who get touchy whenever someone suggests I don't understand what archaeology actually is.

Today I keep my cool and say dryly, "No time for that. And how about you? What's your excuse for straying from the beaten track? Surely you see plenty of the mountain when you go up with Agatha each week?"

"I like the view," he says simply. "Sometimes I just want to take in the peace and quiet on my own." On cue, the phone rings behind him. "Excuse me," he says and steps into the meeting room and shuts the door. I hear him say, "Hi, yes, Marek is just getting Teams up and running now. I know."

I shouldn't listen, but they talk about the new area of fieldwalking. Apparently the project outline specified that Phase 3 was meant to be a preliminary assessment, prior to a separate planning application, but now there are concerns that the quarrying concession has been pushed through as part of the emergency measures. The press secretary is, needless to say, worried about the optics for the PM – the way this will look to the press if this gets out.

It gets out.

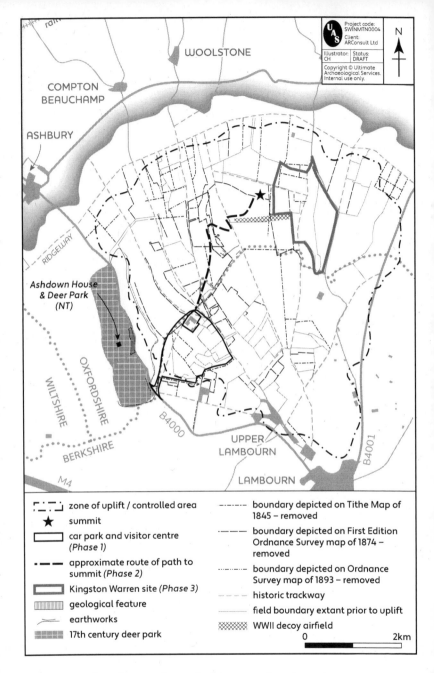

Modern features from the known archaeological resource, depicted on the former cartographic data (scale 1:75,000)

8

This is the statement on behalf of Sir Roger William-Jones:

My client has historically been a donor to the party, but he would like me to unequivocally state that this transient relationship is not in any way connected to the recent application to commence stone extraction on the Kingston Warren site.

The decision to grant planning permission is a local authority matter, and any suggestion of bias or political leverage by my client is strenuously denied.

Sir Roger also wishes me to clarify incorrect reports about his holdings. My client's property within the zone of uplift extends to about 120 hectares of agricultural and equestrian land, of which the majority is tenanted under contract, and a small portion forms the new quarry site. He wishes me to assert that while he and the Home Secretary were both present at a fundraising event for a children's charity in March this year, it was a busy room and my client has no recollection that they engaged in any conversation.

In fact, he joins the NFU in lobbying the government for a practical and sustainable system of compensation for tenants and landholders. His thoughts and prayers remain with the local people whose homes and livelihoods have been affected.

That is all I have to say. Thank you.

A representative for Sir Roger William-Jones

I t's windy on the mountainside. In fairness, it always is. Down there in the valley, I imagine everyone is wilting at the end of a fabulously hot summer's day. Up here, in late July, I'm in danger of getting sunburn on my face while wearing my winter rain mac done up to the chin. It's nice though. The skylarks love it after all that rain, and I think another sort of pipit has moved in.

I follow the sun round the west slope, towards that longed for view of home and suddenly the wind switches off. It's a southeasterly today, so it's been blowing on the horse gallops. I feel sorry for them – the racehorse trainers, I mean. Upper Lambourn is basically a community of rival stables, or it was. I gather from the field team that the trainers have been having trouble getting their horses out onto the tracks. None of the gradients are what they were meant to be.

"Hi."

It should be impossible to sneak up on someone on a mountainside. James's voice has me whirling on the spot.

It isn't exactly a pleasant surprise. I'd been avoiding acknowledging this issue – the way my heart gives a funny little tilt and then a second one upon realising who it is. I sometimes think workplace interactions are something like

Stockholm Syndrome. There's something about being thrust together in such an intense environment that fuels a desperate need to form a connection. None of it is real unless it also exists outside the workplace. And the disconnect between this place and homelife is worse than most.

Plus my car was taken away today. I miss the simple independence of my life of self-employment. At home, I have clients and friends, and rarely they are both.

Finally I spot him, sitting a little way uphill on a block of stone.

"Sorry," he says as I move nearer. "Did I startle you? I thought you'd seen me and would think I was being rude if I ignored you."

Deliberately provocative, I counter, "You're treading a little close to sacrilege, aren't you? Aren't you afraid they'll see you and start a riot?"

"Excuse me?"

I gesture at the lichen marked rock beneath his seat. "Wayland's Smithy is just down there in those trees. It's probably full of pagans at the moment." He's still staring blankly so I add, "You're sitting on sarsen stone."

Ancient magic. Sacred site. Earth energy. The building blocks of Stonehenge and the great portal stones of Wayland's Smithy. The crucial survivor of a thin crust of rock that once covered this whole area and became the key for almost every important Neolithic monument in Wiltshire. Basically, all the reasons why a lot of people hate us.

"Ah," he says. "There's room for two."

He shifts over a little, by way of invitation. I sit. He has his gaze on the sunlit ridge below us when he says, "I was there once on the summer solstice. I imagine it's far more crowded now."

"You went there for the solstice? Like they do at Stonehenge?"

"I didn't go there *for* the solstice. I went for a walk with my girlfriend at the time and it was only when I discovered the place full of druids and pagans that I realised what day it was. It was a while ago. Have you ever been?"

He's sitting in a very relaxed way. I see the slight turn of his head as he casts the question at me.

I on the other hand am sitting very neatly on my little portion of stone. "I've been."

"Then you'll know what I mean when I describe a half-dressed man standing on top of the burial mound, actually upon the capstone over the burial chamber, swaying mystically and weaving his staff above the ground while he communed with ancient powers. He tossed the staff in the air – for the benefit of those of us who classed as unbelievers, I think – fumbled the catch in a stoned sort of way, dropped it, hastily snatched it up again … and then seamlessly resumed his mystical swaying as if nothing had happened. And they wonder why archaeologists speak scathingly of the distance between Neolithic culture and modern paganism."

He seems to realise that sounded unfair. "I don't deny his right to stand there waving his magic staff."

I'm hesitant to reply here. I actually have all sorts of ideas of my own about the way people were in the past, but airing them before the scientists who are actually qualified to talk about these things is usually a mistake. Archaeologists dig these sites. I can only read about them. As a layperson, I know I tend to have a more emotional approach to the past. I think of those people like a story with wants and wishes that can be understood if only I flex my imagination hard enough – which perhaps explains how I moved from archaeological illustration into freelance book illustration. And I will never, ever manage to use all the right terminology.

In this instance however, there is nothing to hide anyway. I'm surprised by my honesty when I admit, "I never seem to be able to quite get my head around the Neolithic."

"The timeline? Or the way of life?"

"Both? I've always treasured the small things – drawing an Iron Age storage jar and finding a hand print the same size as mine; a Roman knife handle intricately carved in Germany but retrieved, broken and discarded, from a ditch in Gloucester; drawing a flint arrowhead so cleanly made I can see the order in which the flakes were knapped. All those handmade objects – they all speak to me. It's like catching a glimpse of someone familiar. But these bleak monuments," I gesture at the cluster of trees below us, "their secrets are too intangible for me."

He doesn't understand of course. He says sympathetically, "It is a bit incongruous when it's hemmed in by trees now. It's probably hard to get an impression of how opposite everything was before – with a cleared hilltop and wooded valley, I mean. It was meant to be visible."

I shake my head. "I understand all that. I understand that it took years to build. I know that a community of people must have spared an incredible number of hours to move earth and stones into a great heaped burial mound. I know that sometimes they buried multiple bodies, and sometimes none. And sometimes they collected up a quantity of bones over a long period of time and then placed bits of them together in a jumble in a chamber.

"I know these mounds were carefully constructed on the summit of the high ground – or at the shoulder just slightly lower down – so that they could be seen from the valley floor. But they were more than a blip on the ridgeline. Some were designed to be white stone gleaming on a turf hillside, and others were a turf mound on an area of stripped ground. Their purpose was to be *seen*. I know all that."

"But …" he prompts. His encouragement is gently mocking. "I'm curious you see, because you've obviously thought about this rather more than your opening statement implied."

I shrug sheepishly. I know I'm talking too much. Yet again. "Perhaps it's your fault that I can't connect to the Neolithic." When he raises his eyebrows, I add, "People like you. Archaeologists."

"Oh. Of course."

"Perhaps it's because prehistoric sites have been so thoroughly excavated and restored. I think I see the modern repairs holding the stones in place, rather than the magic."

I sigh and shift in my seat. Then I add, "Sorry, it isn't that. It's because it's all about death. I can't get past the fact it seems to be about territory, and they're using *death* as a marker post – it's like a giant *Keep Out* sign. It's so …" I struggle for the word, "hostile."

This is the truth of it. I can grasp that the general theory seems to be that they were using the power of their ancestors to cement their claim on the land, and this power could be strong enough to matter to the living. But I can't visualise the individual people involved. I can't make out their rituals. They feel like a story I ought to know, and yet can never quite remember.

"There's one on the high ground over there." He points at the ridgetop on the easternmost flanks of the Cotswolds towards Oxford. "From there, you have an almost perfect view south to this ridgeline, and northwards into the long barrows of the north Cotswolds. It's also placed in the only position where it can equally be seen from its nearest valley floors."

"Did you excavate it?"

He laughs. "No. I wasn't around in the 60s or thereabouts. It just fell within the search area for an assessment I did back in the days when I worked in Oxford."

"There's one not far from my home. I haven't seen it, but it's on the maps." I squint at the horizon – the truly high point, where my home is, near the place where the escarpment drops away to meet the River Severn. I look askance, as if the distant hill is offending me by not giving any answers.

He says, "I like to think of them as great big *we're over here* signs. Over there some other community is answering back – and if you look carefully, there's another one over there … *We're over here!*"

That makes me smile. When he says it, it's easy to think of these different prehistoric communities all standing on opposing hilltops flashing newly formed earth-and-stone beacons at each other.

Then the warmth fades from my face. Workplace

interaction indeed. It isn't fair that I have to like him.

It takes me a while to notice that he's glowering in his turn, but not at me. His eyes are fixed on Wayland's Smithy. "Of course," he says, "all of this gets turned on its head when you suddenly place a mountain beside the scene. That thing down there – it isn't on the high ground any more."

"No. It does rather fly in the face of what we expect from a hilltop monument."

Silence.

I ask tentatively, "Are you all right?"

"Of course." He turns his head. "That's a slightly unexpected question."

The easy quality of his reply makes me ask rather more abruptly than I need to, "Are they still camped outside your home?"

"Worried I'm living under siege while you enjoy the prison-like tranquillity of holing up here? Don't be. It's fine."

I must have looked sceptical, because he says clearly, "I'm fine. I spoke to the press and they agreed to back off a bit. Besides, I've moved back into the tiny boxroom of my boyhood in my mum's house, and I defy anyone to get past her."

Someone starts speaking loudly as they troop along in a small crowd on the footpath down on the ridgeway. We can hear them so clearly, it makes us both jump.

Watching them, I ask, "Does the Seven Barrows cemetery over by Lambourn extend into the quarry site?"

He turns his head. "Why do you ask that?"

"No reason. Ben says there are some interesting circular footings beside an area of scree. And Kate says half the field team are convinced they're going to re-dig some Bronze Age round barrows that were already excavated in the 70s and they've just moved due to the uplift, and the rest are convinced it's a new and authentic area of activity for the altitude – I'm in their camp; I vote for the second option. I'm waiting for someone to come back at the end of the day with proof they've found an upland settlement like the famous one on Dartmoor, with a bit of really juicy dating that clinches the deal."

"Sounds as if you know more than I do. I should be asking *you.*"

"They talk about you too."

"Oh yes?"

"You've got a reputation for demanding more boreholes. They say the quarry site will be a honeycomb by the time you're finished with it."

He laughs. "Well they *are* the best method of producing datable material without invasive groundworks. Whatever it takes to get it done."

He says it carelessly but I'm reminded of his phone call the other day – *I'll get it done.* After a moment, I ask, *"Are* you all right?"

He hesitates. "No," he says. "Not really."

Oh.

"I'm sorry."

He casts an unseeing gaze out over the ridge and into the valley bottom again. Whatever he sees, it isn't the red-tinged hilltops of home. "Sometimes, I don't know what I'm doing here."

I give a short bark of a laugh at that. I can't help it. "Well

I don't think any of us knows *that."*

The walkers have gone and that skylark is rising again. The view northwards is spectacular. His gaze has returned to Wayland's Smithy.

Whereas I'm watching him, not the landscape. And it's a bit like bumping into a colleague in the supermarket. You're either completely intruding upon their lives, or you realise you know them really quite well. He isn't remotely all right.

With his gaze on the offending long barrow, he says, "If they're meant to be on the high ground, it rather puts paid to everything we're doing to manage this place, don't you think?"

He plucks up a blade of grass and begins shredding it. "That pile of rocks and soil is a site of international significance. It has protection. We mustn't damage it or alter it in any way. And most vitally of all at this moment – we must *preserve its essential setting.* But how will I ever be able argue for the preservation of anything now, least of all a lesser site, when the very existence of this mountain changes *everything?"*

Finally, the meaning of what he's saying strikes me. "They're putting you under pressure to hurry something through on the quarry site, aren't they?"

He turns his head. "Oh, they always do that. Thankfully, I'm merely tasked with advising on methodology. Although admittedly, it's unusual for their requests to be accompanied by a personal memo from the spokesperson for the PM."

There is amusement in his gaze. And then I'm hiding a smile too, although mine is rather wry. My theory about archaeologists is correct – there *is* a sense of far horizons in the depths of his eyes. I'm about to ask him what's really troubling him, since the day-to-day pressure of his job clearly isn't it. Then he seems to check himself with a jolt. "We shouldn't really be talking about this."

It's a very managerial thing to say.

He means me to remember that we aren't really friends, I think. It makes my retort rather stronger than strictly necessary. "I don't see why not. Every decision you make will come across my desk in the next day or two – when I prepare the site plan that plots the fieldwalking results onto your proposed locations for the trenches."

More silence, and suddenly I wonder if his point isn't solely to remind me that we have different responsibilities. The rumour that we have a mole flits across my mind.

The thought becomes even stronger when he says, "So, what else have the field team been telling you?"

I don't want to have to wonder if he's asking because he suspects I'm the source of the leak.

I certainly don't want to have to suspect he's asking because *he's* the source.

Either option is appalling.

I deliberately suppress my disgust by saying cheerfully, "I have my own theory about this mountain. Do you want to hear it?"

He doesn't tell me that he *doesn't* want to hear it.

"I think the mountain has been here all along, on and off, but we've just chosen not to see it." I catch his eye. "Yes, really. It's like the time I discovered my horse was afraid of water."

"This mountain is like your horse?"

65

I give a *tsk*. "He's water phobic. When I first had him, we used to go out for a hack about the country lanes and wherever we came across a big puddle in the track, he wouldn't go through it. Made for some very interesting detours. You'd think I was asking him to walk through a brick wall. He simply *couldn't* go through it."

"Was it the reflection? If he couldn't see beyond the surface, maybe he was afraid it was a bottomless well."

"I don't think so. It wasn't simply a case of overcoming a bit of stubbornness. Or at least it wasn't for me. I couldn't even get him to *look* at the puddle; I certainly wasn't able to bully him through it." I hesitate, searching for the right words. "It was as if, for him, the water didn't exist."

The man beside me is nodding as if it makes perfect sense, which it clearly doesn't. He's probably remembering that he said I don't talk like an archaeologist. Even I have to admit he might have a point this time.

But all the same, I'm smiling at the memory as I add, "I realised that if I was going to get him to walk through a blasted puddle of only an inch or two deep, I would first have to get him to acknowledge it was there. So I trained him to look at the puddles first. Once he'd mastered that, I got him to acknowledge that he was perfectly capable of stepping *over* a smaller puddle. And after he'd done that a few times, he clearly couldn't pretend it was an invisible obstacle any more – so then after a great deal more perseverance, I was able to ask him to get his feet wet and step through a wider puddle. And he did it. Reluctantly, admittedly, but he did do it. The key, though, was getting him to admit it existed in the first place."

"You could be describing quantum mechanics. Quantum entanglement."

"I don't know what that is?"

"For your horse, the water was both there and not there. Think of it being like Schrodinger's Cat. It's the idea that something can exist simultaneously in two or more states until it is observed. In his case, the water didn't definitely become a liquid until he finally looked at it." James considers this for a moment. "It's a good theory for the mountain, actually. It was both here and not here until we observed it."

"Oh," I say in a soft breath. "I *like* that."

A tiny spider is climbing up my sleeve. Bending, I transfer it to a blade of grass before admitting, "But actually, I think my idea was slightly different? It relates to the fact scientists believe horses have a mechanism for turning off their awareness of pain. You see, horses have a capacity to keep running, even when they've been horribly injured, because survival in the wild depends on running even if it hurts. *I* think horses have the same knack of forgetting to see something which really terrifies them. I think my horse genuinely couldn't see the puddle until I taught him to look again."

"You're suggesting that humans have somehow – collectively – taken such a fright that they've turned off their ability to see the mountain?"

"I think it might have been there all along. I think we just forgot."

On an impulse, we both turn to look up at the mountain. It's still there.

After a time, he says, "And what does your theory say

about the long barrow? Which research would tend to say was built on the ridgetop …"

"If we couldn't see it, maybe they couldn't either. Or maybe we're wrong about long barrows."

"Sure," he says in agreement, which is all I need to see to be convinced he doesn't believe me at all.

It prompts me to retort, "Anyway, how does the long barrow fit with *your* quantum theory? If the whole being both here and not here principle depends on someone coming along to observe it, wouldn't they have seen it back then?"

He winces. "I have to admit that quantum theory usually operates on a rather smaller scale. Physicists are generally trying to measure the state of a particle."

I laugh. "So something the size of a mountain would be a bit of stretch then."

"A bit." He lifts a hand to rub the hair on the back of his head. "Earth would get pretty chaotic, wouldn't it, if any one of us could witness a new landmass into existence at any moment. Whole cities winking in and out of view, while somewhere else, a bunch of other people are giving us two moons; no, five; no, nine. Actually, none."

He seems to retreat into his thoughts for a moment. "Of course, if we can overlook a mountain, I suppose you could argue it's logical to assume there may be other things we can't see as well …"

"Such as?"

"I don't know. What's missing? Extra planets in our solar system? The lost city of Atlantis? Or—"

"— dinosaurs. Maybe they never died out. Maybe they've been roaming these lands all this time. Maybe that's what makes the hairs on your neck suddenly stand up for no real reason at all as if something very big has just walked past. You can sense them. You just can't see them."

He looks at me sideways. "You embraced that suggestion rather quickly."

I grin, saying nothing. It's thanks to all those winter nights on my own putting out hay in the horse field. Long before all those people caused a ridiculous fuss about the coral fossil, I was familiar with that primeval sense of being prey, that inexplicable sense of being at a disadvantage in the dark, eyes drawn wide, imagination working in overdrive, unable to see *anything*.

I say more sensibly, "I'm doing a bit of homework rectifying the locations of the known archaeology, field by field, onto the new mapping. It was already done at the pre-planning stage by the consultancy team, but I do things slightly differently. I think I can help plot where we can expect to find the same features up there ... and when they're uncovering an entirely new piece of archaeology. Inevitably, I'm also hoping there might be proof in there somewhere that the mountain has drifted in and out of focus before this – but did you know that the really old maps – the ones from the 1700s which just show roads and townships and a gorgeous set of peaks to illustrate the area of the downs – they're wobbly enough that they match just as easily to the recent topographic survey of the mountain as they do to the original pre-mountain OS map?"

His brows lift at that. I think I've finally surprised him.

But instead of passing comment, he only asks as he climbs to his feet, "What was your horse's name?"

"Bart. He's called Bart."

My horse is big and orange and living a contented retirement in his old age with his friends. He also remains the most significant relationship of my life, besides my parents. But I decide James *really* doesn't need to know that.

I watch while he steps away. He's checking the time on his phone. "Are you going to walk further?"

I shrug. "I always give the field staff their space when they first get back. Never get between a hungry archaeologist and their dinner."

"More horse wisdom?"

"Certainly." Then I realise it's more than stupid to stay out here just to avoid the embarrassment of turning our casual meeting into a friendly walk back with him. I get up and follow him down the narrow sheep track.

As if it's a continuation of what we were discussing just now, he asks, "You haven't managed to stretch your evening walks up as far as the summit yet?"

"No. Somehow I think attempting a three hour climb on a deserted mountainside without even being able to tell anyone where I'm going is taking my thirst for adventure a little far. Plus the hour or so down again before nightfall, or a storm rolls in or something."

"Perhaps you should ask David to add your name to the list of bodies joining our site visit next week. He could send both you and the environmental team up with us. Agatha won't mind."

"Perhaps."

When I leave him some fifteen minutes later by his car, I'm very aware of the hollow feeling I get when a snatched moment of companionableness ends in this place. I'd call it longing – I'm always hoping to find a connection here – but I think it's closer to shame. I can't help knowing I talk such nonsense.

With that in mind, I'm quite proud of myself when I only manage to say in an indifferent sort of way, "See you after the weekend."

"Next Tuesday I think. See you Clare."

I turn away. Then something like a cough calls me back. He's bending to unlace his boots and there's something in the way he's keeping his head down that gives me the awful suspicion he's wrestling with the urge to caution me about my pet project and remind me that I shouldn't be moonlighting with company equipment.

"Thank you for talking to me at the end of a bad day."

He finishes unlacing his boots and straightens. "See you next week," he says.

9

Extract from the Scheduled Monument Official List Entry for Wayland's Smithy:

Long barrows were constructed as earthen or drystone mounds with flanking ditches and acted as funerary monuments during the Early and Middle Neolithic periods (3400–2400 BC). They represent the burial places of Britain's early farming communities and, as such, are amongst the oldest field monuments surviving visibly in the present landscape ... [It] is probable that long barrows acted as important ritual sites for local communities over a considerable period of time. Some 500 examples of long barrows and long cairns, their counterparts in the uplands, are recorded nationally ... Wayland's Smithy chambered long barrow is a well known, much visited and outstanding example of the Cotswold Severn style of Neolithic funerary monuments.

[The] Neolithic chambered long barrow known as Wayland's Smithy ... was built over an earlier wooden and earthen funerary chamber.

The main focus of the monument is a partially reconstructed stone-faced chalk mound 56.4m long and up to 13.1m wide with a facade at its south end. This faces south and consists of a dry stone wall against which are set four large sarsen stone orthostats which stand up to 3m above present ground level. In the centre of this face is located the entrance to a narrow stone-lined passage 1.8m high which runs 6m into the mound. This passage has two small side chambers which have a cruciform plan. The remains of at least eight partial skeletons were found when the mound was first excavated, although disturbance of the chamber in the Roman period probably removed the evidence of other primary burials.

The mound [outside] is edged by sarsen kerb stones c.0.3m high and a low bank of rubble set against their inside faces. The mound itself is formed of chalk rubble and turf. Flanking the mound, but no longer visible at ground level, are two quarry ditches from which material was obtained during its construction. These were deliberately infilled in antiquity and survive as buried features 56m long and up to 4.5m wide. They are separated from the mound by a berm c.8m wide. Partial excavation of the site in 1963–4 identified a second, smaller, earlier mound beneath the visible barrow. This mound measured 16.5m long and 8.2m wide and excavation showed it to survive to a height of 0.9m incorporated into the make-up of the later mound. Originally, however, it would have stood up to 1.8m high. This mound was revetted by a kerb of sarsens c.0.9m high which were leant against the side of the mound, rather than being set into the ground. The mound itself consisted of a basal cairn of sarsen boulders c.0.3m in diameter on which chalk taken from the two flanking ditches was placed. These survive adjacent to the earlier mound but are buried beneath the larger later mound. These measure c.17m in length and up to 3m wide.

This cairn covered a complex mortuary structure set on a sarsen pavement 4.9m long by 1.5m wide. Large posts were placed at the northern and southern ends in 0.9m deep postholes and stone banks were built on the east and west sides. A ridge pole was socketed to the two posts, and sarsen slabs and timber (laid horizontally) formed an enclosed tent-like chamber 1.4m high. This contained the skeletal remains of at least 14 individuals, mainly youths but including a child of about nine years old.

For the full List Entry, visit
https://historicengland.org.uk/

List Entry Number: 1008409

Date first listed: 17 August 1882

County: Oxfordshire

My additional reading reveals that of those fourteen early inhumations, most were male but, unusually, two were female. Some died by violence, some not. It could have been war; or famine; or disease. The first monument took a generation to build, and those interments took place over a matter of only a few years. When they closed it a long time later by capping it with a mound, the people who had built it would have been long dead.

Its successor, the long barrow I can see on my evening walks, was constructed in stone and turf in the Cotswold tradition. They placed it precisely where it would be most prominent. Viewers from the valley floor must have been able to raise their eyes to the skyline and feel daunted. It was also constructed late. By the time they built it, they were already lagging 200 years behind the fashion of the time. Perhaps they felt their way of life was under threat and this was their last stand.

In some ways, I feel ashamed that I'm having to work so hard to connect with these people. I'm almost certainly overcomplicating things. I could probably make a simple comparison to medieval churches. These also stand as vast and enduring landmarks in our landscape. Churches are designed to be seen from far away, dwarfing everything around them and reaching ever closer to the sky with towers and spires. They also define a territory – a parish – and have an undeniably powerful relationship with death.

But for no better reason than instinct, my imagination resists the urge to apply a Christian gloss to the rituals of Wayland Smithy. To me, churches belong to a kind of lowland tradition – they huddle in the sheltered places alongside their settlements, and they are visible landmarks so that the living may be called to them and enter them, as well as the dead. It is not for nothing that churches are called the house of God.

The placement of a long barrow on the high ground is echoed in its upland counterpart, the long cairn. I've only set out to learn about the long cairn so that I can understand what made a Cotswold long barrow identifiably – well – Cotswold. But the characteristics of an upland long cairn are fascinating. It would be a burial mound or chambered cairn built out of simple stone on or near a mountain summit. Defying my confusion about Neolithic culture in general, I have to admit that my mind slides easily into imagining the power of a place that hangs high above the world, somewhere between life and death, barren and inhospitable and yet beautiful.

The charismatic high peaks across Wales are studded with them. They have to be less about territory and more about emotion, surely? How can they be about intimidating the neighbours when they require a feat of endurance to reach them and they can barely be seen from the valley floor, except on a clear day, and by someone with exceptionally strong eyesight?

Returning to Wayland's Smithy, like a litany of ancient magic, I see that word over and over again: sarsen ... sarsen ... sarsen ...

It seems strange that later people hardly gave this long barrow a second thought. 100 years later, it lay abandoned, and some 3000 or more years after that, its boundaries were truncated by heedless Iron Age and Romano-British farmers. It wasn't until the early medieval period that it was recognised and once again raised in importance.

I suppose, when I'm searching for traces on the historic maps, I'm looking for a similar trajectory for our mountain. If it existed at all, then at some point, despite all the generations who overlooked it, perhaps some previous person like me will have recognised its importance enough to note it.

10

We've received a copy of an archaeological report that was published in 2004. It shares details of a watching brief undertaken by archaeologists ahead of an extension to the all-weather horse gallops on the slopes above Upper Lambourn. It contains some unexpected surprises.

My guest today is local historian Barry Smith who is here to help explain the details. So, Barry, what can you tell us about the area they call Kingston Warren? I gather the quarry site includes a Second World War airfield? What about the extensive Bronze Age barrow cemetery nearby? And is there information in this report about a little-known Stone Age burial site – not Wayland's Smithy, a smaller one – which yielded the oldest known remains from a long barrow in Britain?

Are we at risk of losing a vital portion of our nation's heritage forever?

Jonathan Clarke, radio presenter, Swindon

I don't really believe dinosaurs roam these hills, by the way, any more than I believe my theory about the mountain. I know they aren't real. It's just a story I tell myself. But it's also a little bit like the feeling I had after I read *The Hobbit* and then *The Lord of the Rings* for the first time as a child. I knew it was fiction, and yet I couldn't ever quite shake off the shift in my mind that merged those stories with other pieces of folklore and told me it was a genuine piece of history.

Today the misty mountains are very close to hand. The cloud is so low, the world outside my office is a white blind.

I'm sitting at my computer on a Sunday with the intention of either messing about with old maps or using work equipment to answer private emails from anxious clients who are worrying about their deadlines. Instead, I'm actually just finishing a messaging conversation with my friend who is looking after Bart and has sent a silly picture of him peering down his nose at the camera – so now I'm feeling incredibly homesick. As a distraction, I strayed a while ago into googling the definition of selective amnesia. That led me towards collective amnesia, and from there I fell down a rabbit hole of ideas, and now I'm asking Google 'is there a term for selective blindness'.

Google informs me that the term is *inattentive* blindness:

A psychological condition where a person doesn't see the things that are right in front of them because they are distracted by something else.

With somewhat appropriate timing, Kate uses her key fob to open my door. They take security reasonably seriously here – the site cabins have electronic locks. I think they mainly installed them to keep the old farmer out. He had a tendency at first to wander around and let himself in to corner whoever was present with a long reminiscence. To be honest, he's one of the most interesting people here, but I can see what it was considered an obstacle to work. Not to mention a sign of lax security.

Kate doesn't seem impressed to find me here. "What are you doing hiding in here in the middle of a Sunday? You can't be working, surely?"

"Nothing much. Just emails."

She steps in and the door clicks shut behind her. She's looking at the plans pinned to the wall, although she must be pretty familiar with them since they outline the work she's doing on site. I send the computer screen to sleep. "What do *you* think the archaeology proves about the age of the mountain?"

Kate rolls her eyes. "I think it's a load of shit. What are they expecting? That we'll find the mummified corpse of another Otzi in the permafrost up there?"

"But you are finding some things."

"A few sherds of Iron Age pottery near those footings. Some flint. A cluster of shallow pits yielding organic material, animal bone. The expected array of plough furrows and the crème de la crème, a crisp packet from the seventies."

Kate has the careless way of speaking I've come to expect from archaeologists. If you listen to them in the abstract, you'd think they didn't even like what they do. In fairness, I also get the impression she doesn't like me very much either, and that isn't just paranoia. It's mainly because the most she tends to say to me is a friendly hello before either demanding a drawing at some speed or rushing off to speak to someone much more interesting.

This visit is … unusual.

"Iron Age?" I ask. "Isn't there a hillfort just along the ridgeway?"

"Your point being?"

"Wouldn't they have built it on the mountain if they'd had the option?"

"The operative term is *hill* fort. Not mountain fort. Just look at Wales. Plenty of forts and settlements on nicely rounded hillocks with a big fat mountain behind. They're meant to be defensible, not inaccessible."

"Oh," I say. "What about Wayland's Smithy?"

"What about it?"

"Would they have built it on a mountain?"

She shrugs. Then she picks up a geophysics report from my desk and asks idly enough that I'm pretty certain it isn't idle at all, "Was that what you and James were doing the other day? Scouting out the local monuments?"

"*No.*" Infuriatingly, I sound guilty. "I was just walking and bumped into him."

"Just an accident that you met?"

"Yes."

"He didn't go with you on your walk? You met him out there? Near the fence line?"

"He was just sitting on a boulder—" I stop for long enough to realise that her mind and mine are running along rather different tracks. She isn't sniffing out an office romance. I narrow my gaze. "Why are you asking that?"

"Classic way of making 'contact' with a handler, isn't it?"

It's so unexpected, I laugh.

She waves the report in her hand expansively. "Why

would he hang around near a fence which just happens to have a public right of way running alongside it? Did you see anyone on the other side?" While I gape, she fires off a few more questions, "Was he annoyed that you disturbed him? Was he *carrying* anything?"

"There was that one guy who was waving from the ridgeway …"

"Really?"

"No."

She scowls at me.

"Honestly, Kate. I don't think James is your mole."

I know now why she visited me today. She knew I was here. I also see the moment her mind tracks my defence of him and forms a new conclusion.

"He's single," she says.

"Is he?" I doubt she misses the barbed note in my response.

"He used to date Theresa from Oxford. Do you know her? She's on the committee for the IfA." When I shake my head, she adds, "She's great. They broke up last year."

I don't know what to say to that. This isn't being said with any kindness. When I first began working in archaeology, the field teams on away digs had a bit of a reputation for bed-hopping. And not in a thrilling, racy way. It was all a bit toxic. Kate, however, is one of those hardened diggers who has had the strength of character to navigate the pressure with her self-respect intact. Experiencing an away dig for the first time in my life, I don't know what to say that will defuse this.

And my embarrassment gets even worse when there is a

clatter as Ben joins us in the office. "Kate … Clare." He nods in greeting. "What are you two ladies talking about?"

Ben is a fraction older than I am so he probably remembers that bygone era of archaeology too. Or perhaps he's part of the younger generation that moved in and expected to be treated like professionals. Be that as it may, Ben is, I have to admit, one of those people who has always sparked a kind of frisson. I've known him for all my years in archaeology. And for all the time we worked together there was a degree of will we won't we. And yet … he's the perfect illustration of why it is not enough to have a workplace crush. The chemistry has never managed to overspill into the real world. Then I left. And now, of course, some time has passed since we last worked together. Everything is different.

Or perhaps not. From the look he casts me beneath his lashes as he takes in the dynamic in the room, I think he believes we've been talking about him.

Oh, perfect.

After the barest smirk at me, Kate twists slightly so that she can lounge with her back against the map wall making the papers rustle, arms folded, accommodating him. "We were talking about Wayland's Smithy. What do you know about Wayland's Smithy, Ben? Clare wants to know."

"No I don't," I say hastily. "What I actually want to know is whether you've found an upland cairn up there."

Naturally enough, Ben grimaces in the disapproving way archaeologists have whenever I use incorrect terminology. Perhaps not an upland cairn. A long cairn?

I explain quickly, "On the summit? I've read that in Wales, they built burial mounds on the mountain summits."

Kate shrugs. "My first dig was on Orkney. We were excavating a chambered cairn on the edge of a beach."

"Were you at Scara Brae?"

"That's Shetland, Ben."

"Ah yes. Not a mountain site in either case."

"No." Kate looks at me shrewdly. "I'm really sorry, Clare. As you say, Neolithic communities the world over show signs of treating mountaintops with special reverence. A lone summit like this, you'd expect it to be an important focus of activity. But unlike the mountains of Wales, there's no evidence that *this* mountain was the site of any specific ritual practices."

She tells me plainly, "There is no burial cairn at the summit of this mountain."

"Oh," I say, solemnly. There is an infinitesimal pause.

Then I say, "They couldn't see it."

The effect is immediate. Both archaeologists break down into unrelenting laughter. Finally, Ben asks, "Why? Do you think that the neolithic was unremittingly shrouded in low cloud?"

Kate counters this in the same tone. "Well she wouldn't be the first. A friend of mine once told me the Dark Ages were called that because after the Romans left, the climate deteriorated and we didn't see much of the sun. He was very emphatic."

They exchange more amusement at my expense. Then her grin gets turned upon me. "You do realise the mountain wasn't here then, don't you Clare?"

I look from one to the other. "So you both subscribe to the uplift theory? You've seen that the same features are being raised to new altitudes?"

Kate shares a glance with Ben, then shrugs. *"You* clearly have a different theory."

Far too earnestly, I explain about my horse's water-blindness and the dinosaurs and the spooky shadows on dark nights. Ben shakes his head. "Save me from pony-obsessed women. Have you ever thought you're just missing Bart?"

But Kate surprises me. She asks, "What about the man who ran along in the verge when you were a kid in the car? Have you looked into that?"

"What do you mean?"

"You know when you were stuck in the back seat when your family was driving somewhere as a child, you'd look out the window and imagine a man running alongside the car, leaping over hedges and racing around obstacles to keep up. Lots of people have a variant of that man."

"Oh!" I sit up straight, the chair rattles on its wheels. "I did that! Only for me, it was a horse cantering along on the verge." He used to jump run-off ditches and road signs and go to extreme lengths to keep to the grass – because even an imaginary horse needed to protect his legs from hard ground.

Ben rolls his eyes. "Of course you had a horse."

"Shut up Ben." Kate moves away from the wall so that she can gesticulate. She's obviously remembering her own childhood. "Collective hallucination is where a number of people share a delusion concurrently, but independently of one another. At least half of the population have a childhood memory of a man running in the verge – or horse, of course."

"I had no idea." I'm going to have to completely reassess every theory thanks to this moment. "That's brilliant."

"Not to be confused with mass hallucination, also called mass hysteria," says Ben. He's pulled out his phone and is browsing the term. "Fear and panic spreading through a population, as a form of socially spread psychosis. Are you feeling particularly stressed, Clare? Kate? The job getting to you?"

"Begone, Ben," says Kate, shoving him back towards the door, and moving to follow him herself. "That's enough of that."

On the threshold though, he stalls. He fights off Kate's retraining hands and turns and ducks his head back inside. "You do realise this gives us a different spin on your mountain theory, don't you?"

"What?"

"If we accept the idea of mass hallucination, but we're all suddenly convinced a mountain has materialised where no one has seen it in any era before ... then the evidence indicates *we* must be the ones suffering the delusion."

I sag at my desk as the door clicks shut.

No. This isn't fair. This isn't my theory. My narrative is more delicate and decidedly more friendly. Not plausible, admittedly, but rather more enjoyable.

I feel the irritation rise. This is why I've never let the spark between Ben and me turn into something. For all his charm and friendly teasing, he never simply agrees with anything I say.

I turn to shut down the computer and a different thought hits me. Kate came to pry into James's secrets, but what about Ben? I tidy the stack of reports on the desk. He may have just followed Kate to see what she was up to, or come to see me;

but if Ben's our mole and he came here to unearth a fresh story for the press, what on earth could be in this office that he wouldn't already know?

11

A phantom island is a purported island which was included on maps for a period of time, but was later found not to exist. They usually originate from the reports of early sailors exploring new regions, and are commonly the result of navigational errors, mistaken observations, unverified misinformation, or deliberate fabrication. Some have remained on maps for centuries before being "un-discovered"

Wikipedia

For the full entry, visit
https://en.m.wikipedia.org/wiki/Phantom_island

Ben's throwaway comment must have wormed its way into my mind, because I find myself hunting for examples of imaginary mountains online, grumbling all the way. I remember reading an article some time ago on the BBC News about two lost islands off the coast of Aberystwyth. They were dubbed the Atlantis of Wales. They were depicted on a medieval map in 1280, perpetuated for a while but then disappeared. For a long time they were considered as much a part of folklore as the legend of Avalon, the mysterious island that is shrouded in mist and secrecy and King Arthur's last resting place – which is said to have been Glastonbury Tor in the era when the Somerset levels still existed as tidal saltmarsh, although the romantic in me struggles to believe such an inland solution.

There are many maps that depict islands that are truly imaginary – phantom islands – such as an impossible extra landmass Francis Drake swore he'd visited off the coast of South America. An awful lot of them seem to fall in the southern hemisphere, although the Shetland Islands seem to have a habit of moving about and masquerading as imaginary islands all over the North Sea. Of course with better deep sea modelling, it's easier for scientists to state more firmly whether the missing landmass has simply become submerged. Sea levels change, land erodes.

In the case of the disappearing Welsh islands, I like the fact that everyone thought the medieval cartographers had got things wrong, until two university professors Haslett and Willis disputed this since in general the map was considered quite accurate. It's the sort of thing I can imagine myself saying.

It turns out the islands were probably lost to the sea in the late medieval period. I went sailing once with a very elderly friend in Cardigan Bay and as we passed over what I now understand would have been the location of the southernmost island, he described a seafarers' legend that there was once a causeway passing from that part of the coast across to Ireland, lost now beneath the sea. It pleases me to think that the evidence of these islands was there all along in myth and legend, if only we'd known.

I also, needless to say, like the idea of there being a

tradition of islands appearing on maps that are fictitious; and islands disappearing from maps and being deemed fictitious when they are real.

I wish I could find references to a lost mountain. I may have already mentioned that older maps of the British Isles – older than the Tithe Map I've been using for my map regression – tend to only depict rivers and settlements rather than peaks and uplands. The etymology of local place names is no use either. Lambourn is quite clearly named for its river.

Searching on Google for vanishing mountains yields an awful lot of descriptions of haunted summits where people disappear. There are some summits which seem to become invisible depending on the lighting conditions, and the most popular example is Gugu Peak in Romania, but this is just a weather phenomenon. There's even a phenomenon called a Fata Morgana – more Arthurian legend – where mirage islands appear on the horizon at sea. These are apparently a mirror effect where something on the surface is reflected upside down just above the surface.

I am, of course, mainly searching for evidence of other landmasses like our mountain which seem to have drifted into view and are widely perceived to be real once they've arrived.

Unfortunately, a search for phantom mountains only brings up a brand of mountain bike.

And following the Fata Morgana thread, my search for mirage mountains ends up digging up an absurd number of references to a Pokemon game.

Then I hit something. The term for a mirage mountain, it seems, is *superior image*. These occur when warm air sits above cold air and in effect becomes a mirror. People sometimes see entire landmasses reflected in wildly different locations. So it's possible my original imaginary mountain is not in fact imaginary. I may have been seeing a real light effect.

I find that thought quite gratifying.

There is one last optical illusion I should mention. Those three round clumps of trees on the ridgetop have been such an important navigation mark on my horizon for so many years, and yet for all that time I'd never completely pinpointed where they were. For a long time, I was utterly convinced they were the trees near Wayland's Smithy, and that formed a large part of my ongoing relationship with that place. But then I lost my confidence, in part because the same ridgeline and those three clumps are clearly visible from the road to Bath, which is thirty miles to the west and on a completely different orientation. The view from Witney, which is twenty miles to the north of Uffington, was inconclusive because the angle of view was so different. So a few years ago, just as I was plucking up the courage to leave UAS, I decided to try to locate them.

I can now confidently say there's no point going too close to the ridge near Swindon as the view becomes too oblique to see the top. It was necessary to pick a vantage point from an opposing ridge in the Cotswolds, and scrutinise the view through a pair of binoculars with a trusty OS map to hand. There are three prominent hillforts along that ridge. Uffington by Wayland's Smithy, Liddington Camp near Swindon and Barbury Castle to the west and they each have a pretty unique profile – surely it would be a relatively easy task to identify them and then orientate myself from there?

I think I have to blame myself for the recent run of wet summers. Every time I thought I might have a day off and continue the search, the cloud would descend and erase the horizon.

It got so ridiculously predictable that on a train journey back from London, where the line passes near the Uffington White Horse, I peered excitedly out of my window ... only for a rain squall to move in just at that moment and shroud that part of the ridge in a white blur. And as I navigated on Google Street View to the one other vantage point which I thought might match what I saw from home – the Commonhead Roundabout flyover by Swindon – and felt that at last I might get the answer, it turned out that the Google car had travelled there on a day of thick fog. Just that patch though. All the other less useful lanes had been reshot on a clear sunny day.

As it happens, I only definitively identified the location of the three clumps after the mountain arrived.*

* On Hackpen Hill beyond Barbury Castle – much further to the west than I had previously thought.

12

This mountain is classed as a lone peak – joining the rarified list of free-standing mountains such as Mount Kilimanjaro, Mount Fuji and Mount Etna (although we're trying hard to ignore the fact they're all volcanoes).

Swindon Mountain is a phenomenon on many different levels.

Aleisha Fry, TV scientist

I am a fantasist. I let my imagination rule over everything. The first person I saw last night when I returned to the accommodation huts was Ben. Or rather Ben and Charlotte – one of the newly graduated archaeologists – in the shadows of the deserted lounge area, caught in an entirely personal moment. For a moment I was appalled by the discovery that he would be part of that old guard of archaeologists after all, while she's so much younger. Then it grew clear from the way she was speaking that they are a proper couple and have been for some time. I retreated, laughing – silently, but laughing at myself all the same. *I've never let the spark grow* indeed. I have such overblown ideas of my own importance.

Today, I'm scurrying across the bare ground between the

accommodation and my office once again, and the cloud is still so low that I can barely see the old farmer by his barns. He's messing about with a bit of baler twine and a broken door and he looks as decayed as the wood with his gnarled fingers and flat-footed wellingtons. I change direction.

"Morning Albert."

"It's a dry day, isn't it?"

"Is it?" I cast a doubtful look at the low-hanging muffle which is gently misting on every surface even if it isn't technically raining. "What are you talking about?"

"The news. It's a dry day for news, eh? Haven't you noticed that they've run dry on insider information?" With mock seriousness, he peers at the tumbledown farmyard buildings as if we're in danger of being overheard. "Have you caught your spy?"

I shake my head. "I don't think so?" It comes out like a question.

"Perhaps you've scared him off?"

He fixes me with a stern eye as if it's a genuine accusation. He means it as a joke. I'm certain he always means to make a joke, but my mind tilts at the thought of all the times I've disturbed people – James, Kate, Ben – and been interrupted myself of course. Suspicion is an ugly thing, particularly when if it isn't them, there's a chance they think it may be you.

Changing the subject, I say, "Are you tidying up the place ready for the adoring crowds?"

"Eh?"

I point at the newly added baler twine on the old doorway. "That looks like it should be good now for another hundred years."

He squints at the rotting wood. Every inch of this farmyard has its own story – the house will lead him into telling me about his wife who died ten years ago; the smaller barn reminds him of his father who milked forty cows a day in this yard before the war while Albert helped as a boy, which makes the man beside me very, very old. He says shrewdly, "At least a hundred. We've farmed here since 1875 and it was old when I was a child. It'll last a while yet."

I ought to ask him whether he minds all this chaos happening on his doorstep, but I think that might lead him into telling me an enthusiastic story about the archaeologists who turned up out of the blue in the 80s to investigate the Roman farmstead in the next field – telling me again, I mean, when I really ought to be getting to work.

I ask instead, "Do you think this cloud will lift?"

He casts an experienced weather eye at the invisible mountainside. "Haven't a clue."

By the time I reach the cabin, it's raining again and doing a very good job of debunking any suggestion that the mountain doesn't actually exist. I learned at school sometime in the distant past – during a geography lesson on precipitation – that mountains have a measurable impact on their local weather system, redirecting winds and stripping clouds of their load before they've had a chance to pass over to the other side. And years ago travelling as a student I remember camping in a steep-sided valley in Austria between two long mountainous ridges. Our side of the mountain was completely dry, but the ridgetop was lit up all night because a fierce thunderstorm was raging on the other side.

I don't precisely know what our mountain's lonely status means for the local weather, but I do know that the area north of here in the Thames Valley is complaining of a dry summer, while the racehorse trainers at Upper Lambourn are adding waterlogged conditions to their list of woes. The local betting shops are running narrow odds on the summit seeing a white Christmas.

> Clare,
> The forecast for Tuesday is light winds so I've arranged with Agatha for yourself, Steve, Emma and Meena to join tomorrow's site visit. You'll need to wear your hardhat and site boots at all times, plus hi-vis. I trust you have appropriate outdoor wear. An opportunity for you to join the dots, so to speak, between what you see in your drawings and what happens in the field.
> David

Sitting at my desk, I'm struck by two things. The suspicion of who arranged this. And the fact that after all this time, David still thinks I need to understand what we do here.

Actually, I'm not at all surprised by the later.

There is a knock at the door. While I'm twisting in my seat to peer out of the window, the figure – middling age, male – raises his hand again.

I pull open the door with a rattle. "Good morning. Can I help you?"

"I'm here for the meeting." I think I recognise the man

on the step. I think I've seen him here before. He isn't very tall, with short hair speckled with grey. He looks, if it isn't too unkind to say it, like an aging salesman who coasts on charm and a cultured accent. Perhaps he's someone to do with aggregates – a rep for the quarry. He asks, "Is she here yet?"

The low cloud is turning to mist on his hair and the shoulders of his suit jacket. When I stare at him in a blank sort of way, he waves the visitor badge pinned to his lapel. "They said I should come up."

I still haven't processed this. I've never had to welcome one of Agatha's guests before. She's always here early.

"May I come in?"

"Sorry, yes of course." Immediately, I step back and let him in.

He doesn't head into the meeting room, he gets distracted along the way by one of the plans of the works near the summit which is hanging at a jaunty angle from its drawing pin after its encounter with Kate's weight yesterday – so after dithering for a moment while he twists himself into strange angles to peer at it, I reclaim my seat.

"Sorry," I say again, after a time, "I forgot to ask your name?"

"Ralph. Ralph Macallen."

"Would you like a cup of tea or anything while you wait? The meeting room is open, so you're welcome to wait in there."

"I'm fine thanks. Did you do these drawings?"

"I—did." I sound odd. I'm so used to treating everything like a state secret – which it is, in fact. And on that thought, my hand drifts towards the telephone. "I'll call Agatha and let her know you're here."

"No, don't trouble her. She'll be here in a mo." He's moved along the row, still fascinated. "And this green one. It shows the LiDAR survey of the Kingston Warren site?"

He glances at me to catch my nod before turning back to his enjoyment of the pinboard. "It's fun the way it looks 3D. You can see every bump and hollow."

Then it dawns on me that it's Monday, when David confirmed in his email earlier what James had said – the next site visit with Agatha will be tomorrow, on Tuesday.

"Are you sure you've got the right day? I'll call her."

"No, don't call anyone. It's fine."

I blink. When I stave off another question by saying something innocuous about the weather – which now I come to think of it is probably sensitive information as well – he moves through into the meeting room. It's my chance to phone security at the gate – except I've never had to do it before; I'm not completely sure what the system is.

"Is this the plan of the works at the Kingston Warren site?" His voice calls through from the meeting room, sounding disarmingly like he *could* be a rep from the aggregates company. It would be preferable to a journalist on the hunt for a story, or an activist who'd love a real scene. He appears briefly in the doorway before ducking back again. I know which plan he's looking at – it's a large format printout of the topography of the mountain, with the route to the summit marked on and the new blue line boundary of the Kingston Warren quarry, with areas of fieldwalking hatched in. None of which, I'd like to point out, pass remotely close to the Neolithic long barrow that was in the press the other day, nor the known area of the Bronze Age barrow cemetery. The quarry will be further to the north than that.

"It's the whole mountain," I call back. "It's just the site boundaries. They're already in the public domain."

As I speak, I'm typing.

> **To:** Agatha
> **Cc:** David; James; Marek;
> **Subject: Visitor at the office**
>
> Good morning Agatha,
> How are you? I'm just getting in touch to say that I have visitor here for you this morning – a Ralph Mackellen? Or possibly Macallen? Do you know him? He's wearing a visitor badge and he says he's here for a meeting with you, but I realise you normally visit us tomorrow? I've shown him into the meeting room. Can you help?
> Many thanks,
> Clare

Then I log out of my computer so that at least my files are locked away when he drifts back into the room.

"So," he says, beaming at me. "Tell me about yourself. How long have you been in this job – what did you say your name was?"

I stand up. It's funny how logging out of my computer has left me with nothing to do with my hands. I tidy some of the reports on my desk. It occurs to me that my next step should be to go to the kitchen to make us both a cup of tea because once there I can track down reinforcements, even if David and Agatha might have something to say about leaving him unattended to do whatever he came here to do.

Then his voice changes. "What is *this?*"

I twist round to find that he isn't transforming into something threatening. He's staring agog at the coral fossil on my desk. It still hasn't been collected and now it's rather inappropriately acting as a paperweight for some of the geophysics reports on my desk. I actually smile as I explain what it is, how it was found and what the world out there thought it was.

"A coral," he repeats flatly after some time.

"You can see that it doesn't have a spinal channel, or whatever the term is – canal – a spinal canal."

"May I hold it?"

It's harmless, so I let him unbag it and pick it up. The pieces move in his hands like articulated vertebrae. Then I move to the door just as it rattles open and two uniformed security guards step in. Everyone is surprised, but also relaxed and perfectly calm. Even when it is revealed that Ralph isn't called Ralph and he's a trespasser and a journalist. And the guards prove this isn't a military-controlled site – they're just people wearing jackets with a company logo. They tell him that he'll have to accompany them to the main gate, and it's as he returns the coral to the desk and gives it a parting pat that I realise that I'm obviously happy being an informant after all, since I told him all that. He certainly got his *exclusive*. Then they escort him out.

And that's that.

Hilariously, the real chaos ensues later, when David and Agatha arrive.

13

BREAKING NEWS: A man was arrested today at the gates of the archaeological dig near Upper Lambourn after he was discovered trespassing in a controlled area. Reports suggest he was living in one of the semi-derelict barns on site, where a tent, food and laptop have been recovered.

Berkshire Police have confirmed that they arrested a man at that location earlier today, but he has since been released pending further enquiries.

We can now identify the man as freelance journalist Barry Jones. There has not, as yet, been a statement from ARConsult, the organisation managing the project at Swindon Mountain. We'll bring you more on this Breaking News story very soon.

Jon Reed, online news editor

I'm sitting opposite David and Agatha in the meeting room. It's a bit like a job interview. In this case, I feel like I'm applying for the job of the innocent party. Although they begin by expressing shock and alarm at the distress the journalist must have caused – who has since revealed himself to be freelancer Barry Jones of no fixed news outlet – they very quickly move on to the task of getting me to itemise *precisely* why I didn't call security right away, what he looked at, and what I told him.

There is a subtle inference that I generally made a hash of things when Agatha turns her head and whispers to David, "We need to talk to PR about how we can limit the damage on this."

David nods and then turns to me. "All right, Clare, you can step out for now. We'll call you if we need any further information."

Back at my desk, I can hear through the wall, of course. Or rather I can hear the weighty silence I leave behind me while they digest what I said and consider how best to respond, and it's then that I become aware they could genuinely blame me for not raising the alarm immediately.

The voices start up again and they're talking about the little camp the journalist made in one of the barns. They're concerned about how he was finding the information he was leaking to the press, given that each area has a secure door. They aren't linking me to that, but I'm on edge, defensive, waiting for the first real murmur of criticism of my actions today, as if at the first whiff of a reprimand I'm going to march straight back in there and tell them *precisely* what they can do with their ridiculous job.

This is why I opted for self-employment. I'm actually seething because I'm excluded from this meeting by the simple fact of my lesser rank.

Never mind that I don't overhear anything particularly bad. They're discussing how to put the best spin on my vulnerability as a woman working in a lone environment. They aren't even criticising me. But when they have a big back and forth agreeing that it must have been hard for me as I'm used to a steady traffic of strangers going in and out of meetings for weeks, and charitably crown that with a reference to my character – do I have a reputation for being nice but a bit dim perchance? – it is the final straw.

With a violence that startles even me, I'm up and out of my seat. I eye the closed meeting room door wildly. And then I fling myself out of the other door, into the fresh air.

I can't listen to this.

14

I've been told by the police not to give press interviews of course – but what is really happening on the inside of that mountain? Read my new column, exclusively in this newspaper, from tomorrow.

Barry Jones, journalist, writing on X

I don't storm out onto the high slopes. I'm not weaving tragedy and anguish about myself like a cloak, and it isn't even raining anymore when I cross the bare ground and head, first to my bedroom, and then the kitchen when the former looks like a prison cell. I don't stay there either. I'm never in here at this time of day and it doesn't feel like home. It doesn't even occur to me to sculk round to the usual sanctuary of my spot on the slope above Wayland's Smithy. I'm not that stupid. I'm not flouncing off on my own, nor am I actually intending to hand in my notice. I'm feeling a little bit shaken, and I'd really appreciate a cup of tea.

The accommodation block is deserted. Everyone is on site of course. The only other permanent staff in these cabins are the finds team, who handle both the artefacts and the environmental samples. Waving my key fob, I push through the door into the lab.

Meena looks up from her microscope. "Hey," she says as

if I'm popping in and out of here all the time. I like the finds team. It's a bit like visiting a show-and-tell. They always have something new to share.

Emma is at the microscope on the other end of the bench with a pair of tweezers in her hand, counting seeds in a sample dish.

"Hey," I say. "How's it going? Where's Steve?"

"Making tea."

"He wasn't in the kitchen."

"We've got our own kettle, silly. *Steve,*" Emma yells. A distant but mildly rude query travels back from the wet room. She draws breath to bellow. "Make a fourth cup will you? Clare's come to tell us how she managed to get taken hostage by a journalist."

Meena looks up and grins at me. "Take a seat. You'll be here a while."

Emma fixes me with an interrogatory stare. "So how did you feel when you found out who he was?"

"Honestly?" I ask, as I slide onto a stool. "Relieved. I was afraid he was going to be someone who'd ask questions I really can't answer."

Such as an environmentalist who might ask by what right we're defiling this perfect landscape with a car park and visitor centre when we could be leaving it to nature? Or a modern pagan who'd ask why we imagine that desecrating a sacred mountain will enable us to comprehend its secrets – before slightly ruining the effect by adding, did you know that the mountain lies on the intersection of two ley lines? It does, by the way, I googled it out of curiosity.

I don't say any of that. Instead I remark, "I wonder how he

got his stories. David said he's admitted to being the source of all the leaks. Did any of you ever see him skulking about?"

"He spoke to old Albert."

Meena turns to her colleague. "The farmer?" She laughs.

"We all been giving Albert the latest updates, and he's been duly passing it on to the man who was living in his barn. Well, we do all talk to him," Emma adds as if any of us is criticising her for being a gossip with the farmer. "He's a lonely old man and we all worry about him."

"Oh God," I say, covering my face with my hands. "I bet I've been giving away state secrets after all."

There is a clatter on the tabletop nearby. Steve has brought steaming cups for all of us. "So has Emma told you about our amazing discovery?"

I look from one to the other expectantly.

Emma beams. "We've been sampling a ditch in one of the areas near the summit that still retains a reasonable depth of topsoil between the fields of scree. A putative Iron Age ditch. I'll say this for James, he's very on the ball about the environmental side of things."

"And …?"

"The preservation is good so we're finding seeds and tiny fragments of charred wood—"

"— charcoal to you and me," offers Meena.

They wait expectantly. Finally I say, "You mean they were living up there? They had cooking fires? There was a settlement?"

Steve rolls his eyes. "You're missing the point entirely. Let me explain. You *are* aware that environmental archaeology is where the real science is done?"

I nod dutifully. The field team and I record the direct signs of human activity. The traces people have left behind. If we're looking at a sequence of pits, for example, the preliminary dating is worked out using broad terms such as when one pit cuts through another – and therefore one was clearly dug first – and if the field team are lucky, they'll find a few fragments of pottery or other artefacts which prove their date, and I'll draw them to record them for posterity. But it is when the environmental team examines the material contained within these features under a microscope that the real evidence emerges.

Emma says, "When a ditch is cut, it almost immediately begins to fill with mud again." She catches my eye and smirks. "Yes, *mud*. And no, it's not the technical term. Sometimes if a ditch sees continual use over a long period of time, it's recut and the bulk of the deposits get dug out, only to begin to fill in again. Most importantly, each phase of use gives us a kind of a snapshot of what was going on around those people at that time – how they were living, what they were growing and eating. With the right conditions – ie waterlogged – we find seeds, snail shells and insects which tell us about their environment."

Meena reaches for a cup from Steve's tray. She's trying to hide it but I can feel the thread of excitement running between them. They've found something.

Emma adds, "In this instance, the ditch is yielding seed from grain crops, amongst other plants."

"What sort of grains?"

"Wheat? Barley? We've found flax seed capsules and stems in the ditch up there. A source of fibre for textile production."

"Most importantly," says Steve, "flax is incredibly cold tolerant. It's found growing at all sorts of altitudes."

"No way." I'm leaning forward in my seat. Their excitement is catching. "So they could easily have been growing it up there?"

"Don't get ahead of yourself. Flax was present. The majority of the other seeds we found were from wildflowers and wheat. Wheat can be grown at altitudes from sea level up to 10,000 feet."

"What's that in metres?"

"Huh. You child of the metric era. A little over 3000m?"

Swindon Mountain is less than 800m. "So do you mean they could have been growing it up there?" I feel my brows furrow. "Or that they weren't?"

"The wheat and flax prove nothing. They could have been at the summit of a mountain, or down by the sea. But then we get to the wildflowers growing by the ditch. Today, Emma identified wild carrot."

I know I'm looking vacuous. I can feel my brain struggling after such a morning. "Is that easy to do?"

Emma laughs. "Not at all easy. But it's my job. It's found frequently enough in Iron Age samples that we think they may have been using it as a medicine plant, long before the cultivated variety became a staple foodstuff."

Clearly taking pity on my confused expression, Meena says impatiently, "Wild carrot is rarely found about 400m above sea level. Commonly found on chalk downlands."

"*Downlands* being the operative word."

I stare at them. Steve nods, waiting. I put my mug down carefully.

"We think we can prove the uplift theory. Whatever happened since, those plants were almost certainly growing and setting seed beside a ditch the local farmers had cut across the brow of a perfectly ordinary hill."

The mountain wasn't here in the Iron Age.

Enjoying their triumph, Emma's mouth widens to a self-satisfied grin. "Obviously, botanists will argue for decades over the likely range of wild carrot, and there'll always be those who can prove there are outliers from the 400m range theory, but yes. From the point of view of using the archaeological record to prove the origins of the mountain, this is it. We've found our proof."

Finally I blink myself back into life. "What happens now?"

"We write an initial report. David is already talking about writing papers for publication. And of course there'll ultimately be a UAS monograph about the excavations. We're due to finish here in the next couple of weeks anyway."

"We're wrapping up here?" I abruptly lose all self-control. My voice squeaks. I know I look horrified. The mountain is exactly as it ought to be – a new arrival – and now this.

I've never felt so ... disappointed.

"Didn't anyone tell you the finishing date?" Meena is surprised by my reaction. She's instantly sympathetic. "I suppose you haven't done an away dig before, so you wouldn't know." She removes the sample dish from her microscope and sets it on a stack, takes the next one and slides it into place. "It was always going to be over as soon as we've finished the main fieldwork. They always want us to vacate as quickly as possible so that the construction crew can get in and get going. You've seen that they're already laying the path on the lower slopes? But you'll be coming back with us to the office, won't you, so I suppose you'll be with us for a while yet."

I shake my head. "I'm only here for the fieldwork phase."

Now it's their turn to look blank, then pitying as if I've been denied a treat by UAS management. "Oh, that is a shame."

To gloss over that detail, I pull myself together and slither off my stool to return my cup to the tray. "What will they do with your discovery in the short term?"

By *them*, I mean Agatha and beyond her the people who decide what the public gets to know.

Steve shrugs. "Media blackout for now of course. I imagine they'll save this juicy titbit for a bit of positive PR a month or two from now when the public inevitably starts complaining about the spiralling costs of construction. Mainly, I imagine it'll be down to the geologists to argue over the precise formation – whether the limestone genuinely belongs to the same group as the Cotswold oolite, and how and why it was uplifted. And why it apparently did it without so much as a seismic murmur. That sort of stuff takes years of research."

At that moment, the door behind me clatters and David walks in.

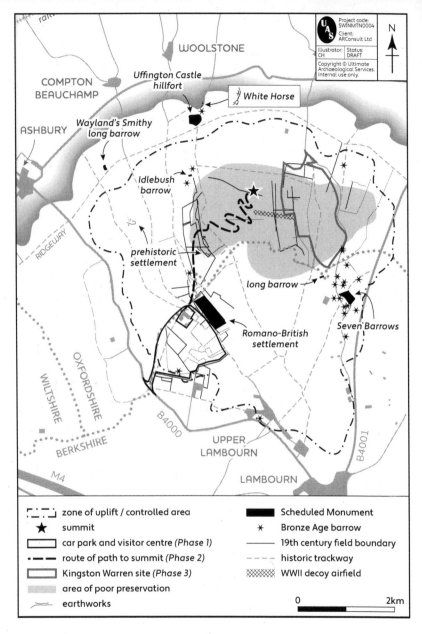

Project code: SWINMTN0004
Client: ARConsult Ltd
Illustrator: CH
Status: DRAFT
Copyright © Ultimate Archaeological Services. Internal use only.

N

WOOLSTONE

COMPTON BEAUCHAMP

Uffington Castle hillfort

White Horse

ASHBURY

Wayland's Smithy long barrow

Idlebush barrow

prehistoric settlement

RIDGEWAY

long barrow

Seven Barrows

OXFORDSHIRE

WILTSHIRE

Romano-British settlement

BERKSHIRE

B4000

UPPER LAMBOURN

B4001

M4

LAMBOURN

⌐ ⌐ zone of uplift / controlled area	■ Scheduled Monument
★ summit	✳ Bronze Age barrow
▭ car park and visitor centre (Phase 1)	— 19th century field boundary
■—•— route of path to summit (Phase 2)	--- historic trackway
▭ Kingston Warren site (Phase 3)	▨ WWII decoy airfield
area of poor preservation	
earthworks	0 2km

*Projected locations of heritage assets after uplift
(scale 1:75,000)*

15

A special train is running between Swindon and Didcot Parkway today. Delighted passengers are set to be carried along the mainline in a reenactment of that old painting of the steam train passing before the Uffington White Horse. Who is it by? Ravelais? This time, of course, passengers have their sights set on a bigger landmark on the horizon. With the promise of fine dining, and a taste of bygone luxury, we've sent Layla Patel along to find out more. Layla, what can you see?

Well Greg, you'll find that the painting you're thinking of is by Ravilious and it's of the Westbury White Horse, but I take your point.

Layla Patel, reporter

I greet David wonderfully calmly. The visit to Meena, Steve and Emma must have worked because I don't seem to be angry any more. David is acting, however, as if this were the strangest place to find me. In the only other staffed site cabin. With colleagues.

"Here you are," he says in an accusatory tone as he steers me out of the lab. "We didn't know where you were. Agatha is waiting for you."

I don't want to explain that I left because I've been able to hear their meetings all this time through the partition wall. "Emma mentioned that we're set to finish here in about two weeks."

"She told you that, did she?" David is an aging archaeologist with a career that left active fieldwork behind a long time ago. He strides ahead in his customary uniform of pale chinos and pale shirt tucked into his belt. Being a true archaeologist in his heart however, he only wears a tie at boardroom meetings. "Well yes, in fact, that's what Agatha wants to talk to you about. We're wondering about bringing you back to the office sooner."

"Sooner?"

He leads me past the kitchen. He is eyeing me kindly. He was my line manager when I worked at UAS. Based on that past experience, I realise I'm not going to like what he has to say.

"There's no real need to have you on site now. The main fieldwork is due to finish here in the next fortnight and this alarming incident has made us think it would be best to pack up your desk and have you iron out the last few details for the field teams remotely from the main office. I don't think data security will be the deciding factor after today's trespass, wouldn't you agree?"

The idea that I'd leave this place voluntarily, today, only to return to the UAS offices raises a ripple that feels like panic, but when I reply my voice is impressively calm. "You want me to come back in."

He's obviously discounting the fact the logistics of going

anywhere at all will be difficult since my car is still with the repair people.

David pushes open the door from the accommodation and steps outside, passing it to me so that I can scurry out after him. "Well it was always on the cards, wasn't it. Now we're just going to speed the process up a bit. It seems the only sensible choice after what happened today—"

"I'm not going to come back into the office."

"— and I'm sure you'll agree it's for the best, won't you? You understand that there's absolutely no blame. Agatha and I are very clear about that. I've always said it was a bit hard on you working in in that cabin on your own. You've coped admirably. And until today ... well, how would *you* describe today?"

That is one of those questions that doesn't seem to have an obvious answer. "Well I can safely say it wasn't a very nice experience."

"And what thoughts do you have about the response?"

I think he's asking if there was anything they could have done better. "I think the security team acted promptly enough. They were very polite."

"And you?"

"Well perhaps I'd call security myself next time."

I mean it wryly I suppose, because what else does he expect me to say, but he nods as if I've been very wise, and it's this that makes me remember that this is his style of management. The gentle manoeuvring into admitting fault.

"But then," I add, "I also remember that it was very intimidating. I didn't know at the time that he was only a journalist. I don't want to go back to the office."

"Of course not. I wouldn't want to work in such an isolated place either. If anything, today's events have just highlighted the fact that site work isn't the right place for you. We were always concerned about your position here, given your lack of fieldwork experience, and weighing it all up, it seems as if now is the right moment to pull you back in. It'll be a relief after being stuck in this lonely place, won't it?"

The question gives me a sharp awakening. I give a strange sort of laugh because it turns out I hadn't stopped being angry. I was numb. Now I'm out of breath from hurrying after him. I deliberately slow my pace. "I'm sorry, David, I wasn't clear just now. I mean I'm not coming back to the UAS office."

I don't precisely know how to describe the currents of this conversation. It isn't far removed from the difficulty of knowing how to handle the journalist. There is a certain feeling that this whole discussion is running on a narrative I can't control.

Particularly when he stops just short of the cabin door and says tiredly, "Oh Clare, I wish you'd said this sooner."

"I *did* say this. Or rather, you knew I wouldn't come back long term. I left! And when you asked me to come back into the office for that other job, I declined. I agreed to do this one for the duration of the fieldwork. I'm sure I said that."

"Well your contract doesn't. It's our standard temporary contract. And you're familiar with what comes next in this project, aren't you? We've got six months of work ahead creating the reports, and three years or more if you want to stay on to produce the glossy monograph after the post-excavation work is completed. I thought I'd put together a reliable team."

That same rustle of panic hits me again. I find I'm watching the pattern the toe of my shoe is making as I scuff the dirt. I feel the edge of emotion in it – this really has been a very long morning.

"I could do the work from home."

"You know we can't do that, I'm sorry." He sounds resigned as if he's lately been dealing with many difficult thoughts and this is just one more thing which is adding to the stress. "The alternative would be to wrap up your role here completely, but what a nightmare that would be. And what about you? I can't imagine you'd be happy handing over the contents of your desk wholesale and leaving the illustration team to pick up your loose ends? Would you? Truly?"

"In all honesty," I reply, "I imagine the illustration team will do what they always do – they'll pick over everything I've done and find all the reasons why they would have done things differently."

In fact, they'll judge me even more severely now that I'm apparently going to incur David's disapproval too. I know this for a fact, because I belonged to that culture when I worked there.

I lift my head. It's particularly strange having this conversation in the desolate emptiness of the compound. Nothing but stark buildings and the intense swoop of the slope above me. It is the weirdest place I have ever known.

"So how about this for a compromise." David draws my attention back to him. "You'll come in for the two weeks while they wrap up the last of the fieldwork, and then you can see how you feel. I imagine you'd love to get away from here to see your horse? Spend some time with Bart, eh? Maybe we can even lend you a company car until you can collect your own vehicle."

It's so reasonable, I catch myself nodding my head. Then I feel my heart race again as I spot the trap. This is a concession disguised as a compromise, because whether he means it or not, I know once I'm back there, it won't be two weeks in the office. I'll feel committed to doing the six months, and then from there it'll be like I never left. I suppose I ought to be flattered that I'm valued enough that UAS would want me back. I'm not after all, if I'm truly honest, earning a great living from book illustration.

"Come on, Clare," he adds persuasively. "I know you wanted to take some time away from the desk, but perhaps it's time to restart your career. I know it hasn't been perfect here, but I didn't have time to recruit someone with more field experience for the role. You know it was the most convenient solution all round to bring you back in."

Not so valued after all.

Perhaps he notices his misstep. His tone grows sharp. "What are you doing here? I thought you wanted to help. What did you come here for, if you weren't going to follow it through?"

"I didn't come here for the *job*," I say, goaded out of calm at last.

Recklessly, I sweep a hand expansively at the towering slopes – or at least the part of it we can see below the low cloud.

"I came here for *the mountain.*"

I stand there, furious and fighting the urge to instantly apologise, while David blinks at me. I don't think he sees what I see in this barren yard of old farm buildings and site cabins and rising slopes.

Although he certainly tries to read the expression in my face. Then he adds bossily, "Well I suppose you know your own mind. You'll just have to tell Agatha that we're going to have to find a way to keep you on site for this last stage. I'm sure she'll understand."

He acts as if it's a huge inconvenience. Which it probably is.

Back at my desk, I don't need to explain myself to Agatha at all. David does that. Opening up my computer, a ridiculous number of emails have come in, including one from James sent as a reply-all to the recipients of my original email.

> Agatha / David, I presume you don't need me to raise the alarm?
> Best,
> James

Then another, with a timestamp sometime later, sent solely to me.

> How are you?

I have no idea how I'm supposed to reply to that so I don't bother. Then I feel ashamed, and spend a ridiculous amount of time analysing the tone of his email before crafting a simple line that will potentially pass muster for both someone who ranks alongside the people closeted in that meeting room, but also someone who may genuinely be asking, in case this is what he means.

> Fine thanks. All very dramatic, but handled swiftly.
> Thanks for your help!
> Clare

Then having sent that, I instantly experience sender's remorse and spend the next hour or so coming up with about twenty different ways I could have phrased things better. It's all a product of shock I suppose. During it all, the mountain hangs outside my window. All I can think, with a sharp pang like heartbreak, is that I have only two more weeks before all this is over.

Much later, my mind clears. I email James again.

> Sorry, what I meant to say was – thank you for the rescue. How are you?

And include my mobile number and the information that I'm on WhatsApp.

16

Let me tell you about the old farmer who lives on the mountain. He's a wise old soul. I first met him when he stumbled out to the barn one evening and dragged me into the farmhouse for a hot drink.

His house is one of the worst affected by the mountain. If you ever wanted proof that it arrived out of the blue, just take a look at his chimneystacks. The whole building looks like it was fine one day and then tilted at an impossible angle the next. No one in their right mind could possibly argue it was deliberately built like that.

In fact, just looking at it made my brain hurt the first time I saw it. Although that could have also been the hardship of living out of a sleeping bag in a rat infested, derelict cow shed.

The cow shed, I should add, was derelict before the mountain came.

But back to kind old Farmer Albert. I'm standing in his kitchen, hands wrapped around a whiskey instead of a much needed mug of tea, listening while he describes his experiences of the mountain arriving.

Did he remember any noises or vibrations?

No, none.

Any bright lights?

Nothing. He simply woke up one day to find that his kitchen floor had developed an incline.

"The odd thing is," he says, "is that I can *see* that getting to the sink is an uphill climb now. But if I close my eyes and make the same route across the kitchen I've made every night in the past ninety years on the quest for a drink of water ..." He shuts his eyes and puts his hands out, miming the act of walking blind across his own kitchen. "It doesn't *feel* any different."

Barry Jones, journalist

I expected the trip to the summit to be cancelled, but whatever wrath I'm bracing for, Agatha clearly doesn't have time for it today. When she arrives, she ducks her head in through the cabin door and says briskly, "Are you ready?"

Now, nearly two hours later, I'm sliding out of the first vehicle in a small convoy of double-cab pickup trucks. Five seats, with Agatha driving and a guest in the passenger seat – who I believe is the head of one of the heritage bodies which will be managing this site – with me, Steve and Meena crammed into the back.

The relief of stopping at the end of our long bumpy drive

is almost painful. I've always said the reason I chose the path of illustration rather than fieldwork is that I wouldn't be tough enough to be an archaeologist. When the engine dies, I can hear nothing. Then the first strains of birdsong rise with a flutter into the sky and then parachute down again. I think they're the same newcomers who have been jostling for position along the lower slopes with the skylarks. Meadow pipits. I remember them from my time in Wales. They're an upland bird.

"We'll walk from here," says Agatha. "Everyone got their PPE?"

She opens her door. Marek, James and Emma, with two men from the construction firm tasked with laying the path are already emerging from the pickup truck behind, white hardhats perched upon their heads. I slide out.

We aren't the summit, not even close. There is no cloud today, only a very slight muting of the blue glare which makes me squint beneath my hardhat. We must be on the south face. The Marlborough Downs roll around us, carrying the distant roar of the M4. Above us, the terrain becomes rougher – patchy soil and vegetation with large areas of scree below short cliffs. The vehicles could have passed through, but that would have meant driving on the archaeology. The route upwards snakes in a curve marked by little temporary posts with hazard tape flying in streamers.

There is a solitary strand of barley growing by my feet.

"I've arranged for the site team to show us what they've found."

We flock after Agatha as she leads the climb to the nearest archaeologist.

Word spread pretty quickly last night that I was leaving after the fieldwork phase. No one really minds, naturally, but still I'm hardwired to feel that I've already put myself back on the outside, even if it isn't true.

"Have you come to see our roundhouses?" A project officer ambles over to meet us. Ian is wiry and weathered to the point that he could be forty-five or seventy, but as far as I know, I don't think anyone dares ask in case he'd have to retire.

He heads over a wider area of ground which has been stripped clear of vegetation and topsoil. It has been extensively recorded with sections and deeper excavations alongside areas which have been left untouched. It looks like a weird jigsaw but it is still possible to make out a partial ring of stone footings, and a drip gully, cut to catch rainfall from a roof.

We gather around Charlotte who is sitting cross-legged and drawing a sketch plan of a posthole. She nods her greeting as Agatha introduces her VIP guest, Helen, but continues working. The field team are used to these visits.

"Iron Age, you say?" Helen asks. More than 2000 years old; and further crude hut circles have been marked out with little flags in the sparse turf alongside the topsoil strip. "Will they be destroyed?"

Ian shakes his head. "This isn't a gas pipeline, it's a footpath."

Agatha explains, "We've got the luxury of being able to go round when something substantial crops up. These excavated footings will be capped with soil and turf and left intact, while the path runs neatly alongside – with a mention on the signboards down at the visitor centre of course. It's all part of the visitor experience."

Which explains why the topsoil strip is wider here. They've already rerouted the path.

Ian smiles. "Steve and Meena, your ditch is way up there, the one that yielded the wild carrot seeds."

Steve follows his gaze. "How high are we?"

"About 600 meters?" Ian has already moved to stand within the centre of the partially excavated roundhouse. "Can you see the hearth?"

At the centre of the circle, a shallow deposit of rust coloured earth has been quartered and sports a stringline – literally a piece of string stretched taut between two little survey pegs which will ensure I'll be able to match their detailed drawings to the GPS data when I digitise them later.

It's pretty sheltered here, in something of a natural terrace. I find myself automatically doing what I always do when I visit a heritage site – I'm building a connection with its people. I'm scanning this group of structures and the terrain, reconstructing a picture of higher walls and neat thatched roofs rising to a conical point. There might be people and animals going about their daily business, and smoke would be running from the rooftops in an inky haze before the stiff mountain breeze carried it away around the curve of the slope. But then it dawns on me with a little twist of something strange that I'm doing it wrong. I need to discount the mountain from this scene.

Ian smirks at Meena. "You're wishing you were out here with us, digging."

"Not really. Because I bet this sunshine is a rarity. What's the weather usually like up here?"

"Last week, we had gusts of fifty miles an hour at this spot, and a steady blow of thirty. Yesterday was … wet."

Helen is looking intently at the footings. "What happens once you cover it over? Will it be safe? How do we stop it from becoming eroded by walkers? Should we excavate the remainder quickly to make sure it gets recorded?"

"Actually," says Agatha crisply, "I think we need James to answer this. Where is he?"

There is an overlong pause while everyone looks around. Finally I speak up, feeling like an idiot. "I think he headed up to the summit with Marek and your other guests."

It embarrasses me that I'm the one who noticed.

I find that I fall into step behind Meena when we continue our climb. She's constantly turning back to take in the view. The vegetation falls away and the summit must be tantalisingly within reach, and yet every turn of the path seems to leave us with more to climb.

Following her gaze, I'm certain I ought to be able to identify Silbury Hill somewhere down there – it's a vast manmade mound near Avebury, Late Neolithic but younger than Wayland's Smithy by a thousand years. They used to think that the mound was a burial site, but its core is a foundation mound of gravel with sarsen stone – that stone again – incorporated at various stages as generations of people piled chalk on top, and now they're pretty certain its most significant meaning was the act of its creation, rather than how it looked once they'd finished.

At some point, the rumour-mill was circulating the theory that our mountain is some outsized variant of Silbury Hill.

But the mountain's origins are geological, not manmade. Whatever anyone would like to believe, this ground beneath my feet hasn't been constructed.

I swing my rucksack down from my back and stop to drag out my water bottle. Taking a sip, I offer it to Meena who declines.

"You're organised."

Then I drag out a treasured chocolate bar, hoarded from the last supermarket delivery.

"Now you're talking," says Meena, taking a piece. "Did you see that Albert has had his moment of fame?"

"No? What happened?"

"He made this morning's papers. Google it. From what I've heard about you and your theories, I think you'll like what he has to say."

When we finally climb up through tattered hazard tape markers onto the summit, the wind hits us in the face like a brick.

Then the whole of the Thames valley opens up beneath us.

It drops away in a spectacular plunge. The basin of the floodplains stretches for miles, hemmed in to the north by the Cotswolds which have transformed into defined springheads and deepening valleys – the distinctive *combes* – that run down to the River Severn, or the River Thames, depending on which side they are. On the far horizon beyond the Cotswold escarpment, if I was wearing my driving glasses I might be able to see a scattering of spiney humps which would be the Malverns, and further west, there's the edge of Wales with the definable shape of the main sandstone summits of Bannau Brycheiniog. It's all there and yet I can't quite connect this view to the scene of my daily walks at the base of the mountain.

After the lesson of trying and failing to reconstruct the Iron Age roundhouses, I think I'm stuck in a loop trying to discount the mountain from the scene.

And I can't distinguish the distant hill that marks my home.

Meena and I finish the chocolate. I draw a breath.

It's hard to take it all in after so much anticipation. It is a proper mountaintop – a narrow area which has seen a lot of footfall with a small stack of stones at the heart and a survey point – constructed by the archaeologists, presumably. I guess we're leaving the marks of our own pilgrimage, since the prehistoric communities didn't build a cairn up here.

It's incredible.

It's ridiculously familiar.

It could be mistaken for almost every other mountaintop I know. The sweep down to the valley floor is comparable to the fearsomeness of the drop from the ridge at Cader Idris, and although these upper slopes haven't yet been handed over to the sheep farmers – the sparse grass is long – this landscape is bare of trees, just like other British mountains.

So far, my efforts to fit the original Ordnance Survey maps to the new topographic survey data have placed the summit broadly within a group of large crop fields, with perhaps just one or two of the historic trackways crossing from southeast to northwest, but up here, I'm not so sure. It's all so different, and there are no real signs in this bare ground of where the old boundaries ran so it's hard to be absolutely certain about my alignments. Further down the evidence was clearer. For example, I believe the Iron Age roundhouses down there will broadly correlate with the area which was marked *prehistoric settlement* on the old maps.

I'm not sure if they've completely resolved who owns the summit. If the mountain has been formed by a simple process of uplift so that what was here before has been raised and stretched, then the old boundaries will still apply. But if on the other hand this summit is new ground, it could have a new owner. Now that the government has decided to run a waymarked path through it, effectively by way of compulsory cooperation from landowners, I'm sure that someone, somewhere along the line, is set to claim an obscenely large amount of compensation.

If they end up rectifying the historic maps to decide the ownership boundaries, I hope they do it *accurately.*

The others are peering over the sharp northern edge where a rippling line of hazard tape marks a sheer drop. Meena and I drift over to join them. For me, it has the feeling of standing on the top of a sea cliff – that sensation where the tug and pull of the wind is strangely mesmeric and like a lure. I've always loved that feeling, and yet I've never trusted my feet or my sense of balance close to the edge.

Agatha makes me jump when she speaks beside me. "We're heading down now."

This is not, of course, a day off. Dropping out of the wind is like turning off a switch. I hadn't realised how much of a scramble it was coming up, but I have to slither down a particularly tricky part on my seat. Perhaps it's because there isn't officially a trail on this side of the mountain – we find ourselves pathfinding our own unmarked route through crumbling outcrops.

It's the sheer physical difficulty of navigating this terrain that makes me realise what has been bothering me the whole time I've been up here.

As I've already mentioned, whenever I visit a historic landmark, I'm in the habit of using my imagination to strip back the modern to reconstruct a picture in my head of what it was like back then. Already, I've dutifully rewritten the story of those roundhouses to build a new scene of a little farming community eking a living on the hospitable slope of a chalk down. Their long field boundary would curve away over the brow to the place where it passes through Wayland's Smithy – and I can see it makes a lot more sense than a fragile community clinging to a mountainside.

It's so unreasonable of them to prove my perfectly lovely theory wrong.

We seem to be flocking over to join the huddle that surround James. We arrive just as he eases into a crouch at the base of a particularly craggy cliff, backed by Kate and Marek, and the representatives from the construction company, who in turn are surrounded by the team who were surveying the summit. They're peering at a dark line in the rock.

"What have you found?" asks Agatha.

The cave mouth is narrow. Perhaps a truly determined potholer could wriggle in on their belly – and probably will, along with every daredevil Influencer who arrives in the first wave as soon as the boundary fence comes down – but really it's just a black horizontal slit in a large step of limestone. The bare shoulder of the mountain rises in leaps and jerks, it looks weathered and inhospitable and the sort of place I would encourage people to observe from a respectful distance. We're standing in a relentless breeze. There's no mistaking the altitude.

James tilts his head at the void as if listening. He mutters something about drums in the deep.

Someone sniggers.

Suddenly businesslike, James dusts off his hands and rests his forearm across his raised knee as he turns his gaze to Agatha. "This is a useful discovery."

"You want to dig it?" Helen asks, just as Agatha says, "I don't think we have a budget for that?"

I catch the glimmer of hidden smiles around me as James gives a shake of his head. He squints up at Helen. "You know that hillwash sometimes fills caves with layers of sediment, right?"

"Years ago, I was involved in the management of Cheddar Gorge." Helen lifts her chin proudly. "I know all about the analysis of colluvium and windblown deposits on the floor of a cave. Archaeologists in the 1900s were excited about the discovery of 9000 year old human bones; our recent study of the deposits built a picture of *a million years* in those caves."

James climbs to his feet. "Well I think this cave will cause a similar amount of excitement in the right circles."

"Why?" asks Agatha. "I thought the mountain was riddled with caves? It's limestone – it's practically a honeycomb. So why this cave, specifically?"

"Because this one lies just below the summit." James scuffs the dirt with his boot. "There's limited soil and vegetation.

It's mainly limestone above this point. You'll have noticed that there is a sort of horizon where the soils and remnants of the chalk downlands fade away and the limestone outcrop becomes the dominant feature?"

He turns towards Helen. There's something in his expression which makes me think of his previous signs of strain. This was what he was afraid of – or rather what he was afraid of missing – his responsibility for the science itself, and the risk of overlooking something. He does not, after all, have a realistic hope of anyone coming back after the mountain is opened to the public to find things in an untouched condition. It won't be long before this natural amphitheatre becomes an equally natural lure for tourists and cavers. It already is, I suppose. We're here after all.

He says, "Lower down the slope, we might argue that the sediments that have been washed into this cave belonged to the original terrain before it was uplifted. But up here, if we're looking for a means of sampling a snapshot of the ecological and archaeological record from a rock formation that isn't supposed to be here, I suspect this cave is as good as it's going to get."

On the opposite side of our group, Kate mouths *boreholes* to the archaeologist beside me. He doesn't notice but then she catches my eye and grins.

"You think this cave is going to explain the origins of our mountain?"

I see James's quick smile. "Well, it's certainly going to give them plenty to argue about for a time."

Agatha interjects briskly, an eye for all the extra ears listening in. "We should discuss this further in the meeting."

I almost laugh at the illusion they have about the soundproofing of that place.

It's a very private joke.

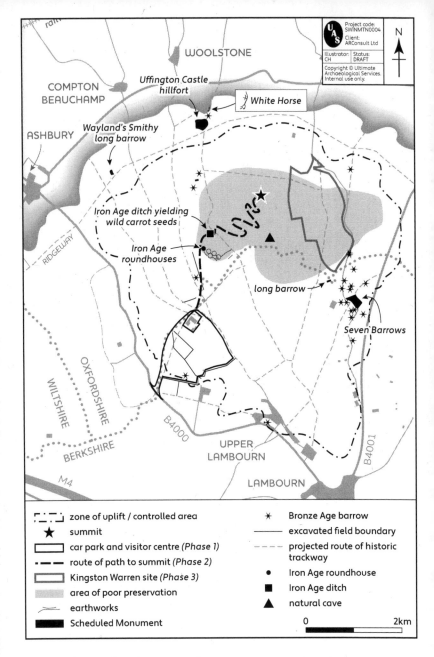

Plan showing preliminary excavation results,
Phases 1 and 2 (scale 1:75,000)

17

We're familiar with the concept that the process of upthrust takes millions of years, and that a mountain may only begin to shrink once the effects of erosion become the dominant force, but researchers at University College London have made an unusual discovery. They have revealed that the world's highest peak, Everest, is *taller* than it ought to be.

It has long been understood that the Himalayan range is still rising year on year through the continued movement of the Indian and Eurasian plates. New research has suggested that the summit of Everest is potentially more than 20m *higher* than expected.

It is thought this discrepancy is due to the erosion of landmass at its base by a nearby river.

Effectively, the mountain was being weighted down by the land at its roots. Now, as the ground at the lowest levels loses mass, and therefore gets lighter, geologists have suggested it is becoming easier for the forces of upthrust to continue pushing Everest higher.

I and my fellow members of the Society want to know: what does this tell us about Swindon Mountain?

Setting aside the obvious geological differences between Berkshire and the Himalayas, the fundamental question is this. Is our newest peak shrinking or growing? It was measured at 783 metres high in February. What will its measurement be next year?

Letter to the editor, British Science Magazine

The day I heard a raven sing, back in the time before there was officially a mountain where Lambourn Downs used to be, I was walking home from the field after checking on my old horse. I climbed up through a meadow towards a tumbledown gateway and it was there, perching on a fencepost, mumbling to itself.

I don't pretend that the raven had the melodic range of a smaller bird. It didn't sing as a blackbird might. But nevertheless, the early summer sun was warm on its back and it was communicating its joy of the day in *song*. They're supposed to simply bark and croak.

It flew off as soon as I came into view.

My experience of this mountain is a little bit like that. I might be here now, but there'll be no lasting proof once I leave. Excepting perhaps my name will appear in a report somewhere along the line, credited for an illustration.

I'm sitting on that slab of sarsen stone again. Wayland's Smithy is just below, screened by the ring of trees that surrounds it. The sky is bright and clear today, so I can also see the sweep down to the valley floor, and cars running along the thread of roads. Something glints on the horizon. Probably another car, passing over the brow of a Cotswold hill. That rival mass of limestone seems closer today and it strikes me in a way that it never has before that our long barrow's placement on the forward slope of the ridge is as much a vantage point as a landmark. It's a place to see and be seen.

Finally, rightly or wrongly, I feel a kinship with its people. They probably stood up here and found this view beautiful too.

"Hey." The man beside me gives a slight nudge to my elbow.

"Hi."

"What are you thinking?"

"I'm sitting here doing that thing where I'm convinced that I and I alone truly understand the magic of this place. And I'm fuming because all those people who will come afterwards will be nothing more than hollow trespassers."

I hear his laugh.

"What about you?" I ask.

"The same. Do you think if we build a big stone mound up here, people will accept it as our territory and keep away?"

After a moment, I reach down to the dirt by my feet. Picking up a small fragment of stone, I pass it to him. "Here. The first piece."

Even as I hand him the stone, I feel a spasm of something that must be guilt for doing precisely the thing I will despise future visitors for. Making my mark. But then it's too late. Until it isn't.

Briefly, there is a touch of warmth as his fingers brush mine. He takes the stone from me, weighs it in his palm and then sets it down, not between us on the slab, but back in the dirt by our feet.

"I think I can live with the idea of consigning myself to being one of the invisible people."

He makes my heart kick.

"If that's OK?" he asks.

"It's perfect."

That being said, we aren't going to be invisible anyway. There's shortly going to be a great white streak of a laid track to the summit, and we helped to create it.

When I say this to James, he laughs. "Yes, but besides *that*."

I can't tell whether returning that small fragment of rock to the earth is genuinely a way of un-marking of our presence, or if I've just forged a permanent tie to this place.

Either way, I came here, and now I'm leaving. A speck of a human life longing for a 160 million year old piece of limestone.

Unless of course it disappears overnight. And we forget it was ever here at all.

What was it I said about relationships? They're only real if they also exist outside the workplace?

I guess I'll know tomorrow.

GLOSSARY

(A GLOSSARY OF TERMS WHICH MAY NOT
NECESSARILY FALL UNDER MY PARTICULAR
SPECIALISM BUT ABOUT WHICH I HAVE
FORMED STRONG OPINIONS)

Geophysics / geophysical survey report: a means of 'seeing' beneath the surface of the topsoil without digging using ground penetrating radar or magnetometers, of which the latter can distinguish between the magnetic response of the natural bedrock and the different magnetic response of any features cut through it. The results will be shown in shades of grey, with the darker tones indicating areas of deeper soil. The geophysicist will usually also provide an interpretative plan which identifies both natural and man-made features, and the potential locations of pits and postholes using the subtleties that my eyes could never spot. These plans help the archaeologists decide where to target their trenches and form reasonable expectations of what *might* be found ahead of their excavations.

LiDAR: Light Detection and Ranging is a survey technique which generates a detailed scan of the surface of the land by sending pulses of light from a consistent altitude (often with a drone) and measuring the time taken to return. These pulses of light are even able to penetrate foliage to the ground below, so the results allow the archaeologists to identify potential earthworks and surface features. Again, LiDAR is used to determine what might be found within a site ahead of any potential archaeological works.

GIS software: Geographic Information System software, used by archaeologists for plotting the results from the field on to the Ordnance Survey Data. I've always found it unwieldy and struggle to give the finished illustrations their higher level of polish. My specialism has tended to be AutoCAD (Computer Aided Design) which is commonly used by architects but is useful for producing accurate drawings in 2D or 3D of a site and its features, and also the Adobe Creative Suite, which allows a much higher level of finished presentation which in turn can help with digestibility.

Map regression / rectification: the process of fitting historic maps to modern mapping data for the purposes of identifying historic boundaries and seeing how they have been added or removed over time. One of my favourite parts of the job, I always took an unreasonable amount of pleasure from successfully aligning a historic map with the present day without riding roughshod over the original cartographer's interpretation.

Finds / artefact illustration: a process of producing a measured drawing of an object using pre-established conventions. These drawings will travel the world to specialists while the original artefacts will be stored in controlled conditions in the archives of a museum, so they're vital for our ability to learn and disseminate the results of our discoveries. Drawing conventions are reasonably fixed so, for example, rough handmade Neolithic pot sherds would feature stippled shading, whilst Roman and medieval pottery would be shaded with lines to indicate that these were wheel-thrown. This allows specialists wherever they are in the world to study and interpret the evidence without confusion. I have particularly good near sight (for example I can see the tiniest facets of retouching and knapping on a flint tool without the need for magnification) and I think this influenced my particular interest in this aspect of the job.

PPE: personal protective equipment for site safety.

Geological column: also known as a stratigraphic column. A vertical diagram of the layers of rock and other formations in a given location, with the oldest at the bottom and the youngest at the top.

Oolitic limestone: a sedimentary rock formed in warm shallow seas. Calcium carbonate forms on the surface of sand grains and other small particles in a relatively calm sea. Over time, the resulting grains (called ooids) are rolled smooth like the pebbles on a beach and ultimate compressed to form limestone. The Cotswolds oolitic formed during the Jurassic era, between 201 to 145 million years ago.

Chalk: a sedimentary rock which is a form of limestone. It consists of the mineral calcite, or calcium carbonate, which is formed by the prolonged deposit of deceased plankton and the shells of other tiny organisms on the ocean floor. The chalk Marlborough Downs formed during the Cretaceous period, roughly 145 to 66 million years ago.

Weald-Artois Anticline: an anticline is a geological fold. The Weald-Artois Anticline is a pronounced geological fold which runs between the Weald region of southern England (mainly parts of Surrey, Sussex and Kent) and the Artois region of France. It was formed during the Alpine orogeny (process of uplift) from the late Oligocene to middle Miocene about 25 to 15 million years ago, and raised the chalk downs by nearly 200 metres. At this time the land formation would have spanned the channel and linked England with mainland Europe. Later erosion led the sea to breach the barrier repeatedly until a final breach about 6000 years ago created the Strait of Dover. The anticline still continues on the ocean floor.

The Marlborough Downs: these lie far to the west of the Weald-Artois Anticline and are considered to mark the southern limit of the glaciers of the Pleistocene Epoch, commonly known as the Great Ice Age. These downs escaped the extreme erosion of the glaciers which wore away the chalk layer from other areas of the region, such as the Cotswolds.

Neolithic: The dating given to different named periods relates as much to their sociocultural practices as their degree of technological advancement. The Neolithic period in the UK ran from about 4300 BC to 2000 BC. Neolithic (meaning New Stone Age) people were the first farmers in the UK. Their monuments are some of the most well-known features in our historic landscape, such as Stonehenge, Avebury and Silbury Hill, along with the long barrows of the Cotswolds.

Bronze Age: This period spanned from 2500 BC to 800 BC in the UK. The dates are not fixed and vary from region to region and as new information comes to light. There were innovations in the Late Neolithic which span into the Bronze age, and likewise innovations in the Late Bronze Age which relate to the technological advancements of the Iron Age. Bronze Age people lived in relatively settled farming communities. They often created large barrow cemeteries, where each barrow might contain several inhumations and cremation burials, perhaps tended in a similar way to modern burial plots. Local examples include the Seven Barrows site above Lambourn which potentially contains more than forty bowl barrows, and also the area of the three round clumps on Hackpen Hill that have formed such a significant landmark on my road journeys.

It seems to me that the people in the Bronze Age may have liked their dead to have a nice view.

Iron Age: running from about 800 BC to 43 AD with the arrival of the Romans. The end date is fixed by documentary evidence, but the start date has been pushed back several times as new information comes to light. It has always seemed to me that Iron Age people lived and worked in communities comparable to our modern semi-urban lifestyles where a person might work to produce an item, sell it, and then use that income to buy everyday staples such as food – rather than subsistence farming where each household is responsible for farming whatever they can for their own survival before trading any surplus for other items. Iron Age hillforts, which in many cases were fortified settlements, may have had many roles from marketplace and defensive through to religious centres. Their distinctive ditch and bank earthworks are a prominent legacy from this era.

The cave in the natural amphitheatre: James is not the only person to make a Tolkien reference in relation to that cave. Social media is awash with LOTR memes reviving the monster myth because we *dug too deep.*

A note on the convention for naming mountains: where mountains are in Wales, the Welsh name is used. For non-UK peaks and mountain ranges, their English name is used for clarity. Future records of the archaeological works for Phases 1, 2 and 3 may include an updated nomenclature for Swindon Mountain to align with our evolving understanding of the site.

"Practically a feminist manifesto for women artists ... a love story about the hidden lives of artists and the urge to create" — as seen in COTSWOLD LIFE magazine

★★★★★ "Definitely left its mark on me ..." "5 stars"

nude
HARRIET HITCHEN
the portrait of a forgotten artist

The hidden life of an artist is told through the work they leave behind. But every painting holds its secrets, and sometimes it's easier to live with the myth than admit the truth ...

ABOUT THE AUTHOR

Harriet Hitchen is a former archaeological illustrator, becoming an accredited Member of the Association of Archaeological Illustrators and Surveyors (MAAI&S). She has a degree in Fine Art, particularly focusing on figure painting. She loves to unpick the emotional stories behind the facts of great artworks and heritage locations, trips to London and exploring rambling country houses. Her first novel *nude* reimagines the secret life of a forgotten Pre-Raphaelite artist. *Swindon Mountain* combines her passion for archaeology with science fiction.

She lives near Cheltenham with her husband.

ACKNOWLEDGEMENTS

The roots of this story belong in the history of my own commute to the archaeological unit which gave me my first job after university. Like Clare, I found the drive in my car over the high ground in the Cotswolds utterly captivating as the glimpse of the distant grey wall of the Marlborough Downs rose into view. One of the first sites I visited when I moved to the area was Wayland's Smithy.

The shadow mountain is real. At the time of starting to write, I didn't know anything about superior images. I had no idea that the brief vision I experienced once or twice a hazy day beyond that ridge could have any foundation in reality. It has thrilled me that in the process of researching and creating this story, I have been on my own journey of discovery and been able to give a meaningful explanation to the experience which first inspired this book.

The plans which accompany this edition are based upon a genuine assessment of the known archaeology of the Lambourn Downs. The alterations I have made to the historical record for the purposes of the plot are as follows:

- The earthworks depicted sightly to the east of the projected path to the summit which are labelled prehistoric settlement are undated on the source information I have used;
- Buildings within the zone of uplift and farmsteads have been erased. The farm buildings described in

the text are entirely fictional;

- Some of the historic field boundaries marked within the area of the car park and visitor centre have been inserted.

It gave me great pleasure to resurrect my former passion for map regression for the sake of this book and so I owe a particular debt to the online resources of the National Library of Scotland for mapping, and Historic England for aerial photographs and detailed information about Scheduled Monuments.

Geological information was pieced together from many different sources. My grateful thanks go to the British Geological Survey online resource which includes endlessly fascinating maps showing the extent and depths of the various formations – I really do love a good map.

In addition, I cannot thank archaeologists Gail and Sylvia enough for providing on one particularly memorable roadtrip so much valuable information about the stages of archaeological work during the pre-planning and mitigation phases. Your experience and expertise is awe-inspiring and you allowed me to bend the rules to suit the exceptional circumstances of this particular site, and helped me to unpick the technicalities of James's role. Any errors in this work are mine alone. I can't wait for our next roadtrip.

To Jeremy Brookes my editor at Crumps Barn Studio, thank you for all your hard work, and most particularly for spotting a niggling detail where I could not.

Thank you also to the archaeological company and the archaeologists who made my first career as an illustrator so fascinating. The company and people in this book are entirely a work of fiction, but all the magic of working with you was very real.

For anyone who harbours a dream of pursuing a career in archaeological illustration, there are many routes into the workplace. Mine was through work experience and volunteering alongside my studies in order to gain enough skills to join at a junior level. Alternatively, illustrators often specialise after completing an archaeology degree, while others diversify from a surveying background. It is an incredibly varied and fascinating field whichever route you take, but I can't promise that the job will include unearthing the secrets of a newly discovered mountain.

The inspiration for Bart and his aversion to puddles belongs to Jack, my beautiful first horse who takes the credit for changing the direction of my life, introducing me to my husband and bravely conquering everything (even water).

My eternal thanks go to my husband for being willing to revisit the high ground in the Cotswolds time and time again in the hope that the light would be clear enough to definitively locate the elusive three clumps of trees once and for all (it wasn't). I cannot believe that visiting those trees in person became such a quest, but I'm so glad that when I finally set foot on the right portion of ridgeway in dense fog with absolutely no view at all, you were there with me.

If you loved this book, you'll love these
other fiction titles ...

Kirin of the Dobunni
Anne Buffoni

AD 8. Kirin is determined to help his young friend find the way back to her family, but they must be careful. There are whispers of betrayal in the face of an expanding Roman Empire. The gripping historical novel full of gods and secrets of the Dobunnic tribe in the last days of Iron Age Britain, with an exclusive guide to the archaeological sites

ISBN 9781915067357

Mr Redmond's Mending Day
Michael Bartlett

This family gathering is more than a chance to lay the past to rest. In fact, the next twenty-four hours may just change everything …
The poignant and tender story about love, loss and the threads that make a family, from the renowned radio scriptwriter

ISBN 9781915067586

Just Causes
Georgia Piggott

Dorset, 1625: Alice Edwards is on her own and fighting for all she holds dear. In a time of deadly plague, hope lies in herbs and remedies. But sickness is not the only danger. The first book in the page-turning historical mystery series, now in a special edition

ISBN 9781915067685

Crumps Barn Studio
crumpsbarnstudio.co.uk